Spoons and Solids

The Ultimate Guide to Baby-Led Weaning That Eliminates Rules, Fear, and Stress

Jocelyn Goodwin

Contents

How To Get The Most Out Of This Book

To help you along your parenting journey, I've created two free bonuses to save you money, time, and headaches. These bonuses are updated in real-time and change as new products and resources become available.

I highly recommend you sign up now to get the most out of this book. You can do that by going to the link below.

www.thefirst12months.com/#bonusblw

Free Bonus #1: Baby-Led Weaning Essentials: tried and tested must-have products that parents love. The complete list of the only baby-led weaning and spoon-feeding items that you need. I ordered over 100 different items over my parenting years, and whittled it down to the real stars. You can trust these products will get the job done. I have considered durability, ease of use, and many other factors, to make sure they enhance you and your baby's weaning journey.

Free Bonus #2: Baby-Led Weaning Cheat Sheet: Printable PDF that includes everything you might want to remember when you are in the kitchen, including...

- True-to-size diagrams on the shape and size of basic foods
- How to form a balanced meal
- Top 8 allergens
- List of iron-rich foods
- List of foods to avoid
- Meal Plans
- 3-ingredient recipes

To get your bonuses, go to:

www.thefirst12months.com/#bonusblw

Foreword
By Krista Jensema

As a pediatric dietitian, I have seen parents confused, overwhelmed, and terrified when the time comes to introduce food to their children. This is meant to be an exciting time! A time to introduce new textures, colors, and tastes outside of breast milk or formula. Recently, there has been a lot of added pressure to introduce purees or solids in the correct way, but there is no perfect way to do so! It is all about finding what works best for you, your family, and your little one.

Believe it or not, learning to eat is one of the most complex skills that humans will learn, because it involves using all our senses at once. Every day, I teach this specific skill to children and parents. I see babies thrive and I also see the potential effects of not introducing foods, including delayed oral development and picky eating later in life.

My role within the field of pediatric nutrition is to help parents provide their children with a variety of balanced nutrients to optimize growth and development. Baby-led weaning (BLW) is a great option for a lot of parents, but I also hear some of the biggest concerns, including time management for meal planning, meal prepping, safety from choking, and adequate nutrition. Many parents are very nervous, but *Spoons and Solids* will provide you with the tools necessary to ease you into the world of BLW with confidence.

Although there is no exact science regarding what will work best for each child when it comes to introducing food, my experience with BLW is that it often results in a greater acceptance of a variety of foods throughout the different stages of childhood and adolescence. Jocelyn has highlighted a large assortment of research that confirms my experiences with BLW, and she outlines a practical and flexible approach for introducing solids.

What makes this book unique is that it encourages parents to do what works best for their lifestyle and the developmental skills of their child. I have had many parents come to me feeling like they have failed at BLW because their child did not show interest in food, or their daycare was not willing to provide non-pureed foods. You or your infant may not be ready for BLW and that is okay! Following a more traditional route of working up to solids can also provide all the necessary nutrients and skill development for your child.

As a dietitian that works with infants, children, and adolescents regularly, I believe this book will give you the confidence and tools to guide you through the messy, tough, rewarding, and often confusing times of introducing food to your child. I have thoroughly enjoyed working with Jocelyn and I have closely reviewed all meal plans, recipes, and meal ideas within this book to ensure they are nutritionally complete for a healthy, full-term infant, when given alongside regularly provided breast milk and/or formula.

Congratulations on taking the first step in your journey with baby-led weaning! You are on your way to raising a healthy and adventurous eater!

Krista Jensema MS, RD, CSP, LD,
CLC Registered Dietitian Board
Certified Specialist in Pediatric
Nutrition

Introduction

When it comes to weaning, there is no one-size-fits-all solution. Your family, your baby, and you are no exception. Despite this oft-quoted proverb, our society continues to try and push parenting into one box or the other. You either have to do formula feeding or breastfeeding, cloth diapers or disposable diapers, scheduled or on-demand feeding. Most of us spend weeks or months trying to conform to these ways of parenting, only to eventually find out that we succeed when we are somewhere in the middle.

Growing up the first of five children, I spent most of my childhood taking care of my brothers and sisters and quickly learned that I loved babies. As a young adult, my free time was spent babysitting and reading parenting books for fun. When I first came across the practice of baby-led weaning, AKA weaning your baby using finger foods instead of puree, I was very interested.

I read everything I could get my hands on and I was blown away by all the benefits of providing solid food right from the start. Although it was recommended by multiple pediatricians, health care professionals, and dietitians worldwide, there were also many skeptics, and there was a lot of fear about choking. Everything I read had differing opinions on the best ways to wean, and I was utterly confused.

After much internal debate, I jumped into baby-led weaning headfirst. I followed all the rules, made delicious recipes three times a day, and in the meantime, drove myself, my baby, and my husband nuts. Since when did feeding a baby get so darn complicated?

I reached out to parents. Some were succeeding, while many seemed just as overwhelmed as I was. Although I loved watching my baby explore solid food and learning new skills, I was constantly second-guessing myself on what was okay and not okay to feed my baby, and my anxiety around meals increased. With our busy schedule, I thought, *There has to be an easier way to do this!*

Over the next few weeks, I took what I had learned from baby-led weaning and transferred it to puree feeding. I started experimenting with how I offered purees so that my daughter had more control. I would wait for her to open her mouth before I placed the spoon in it, and I let her remove its contents on her own.

Within a week, weaning became enjoyable instead of something I dreaded. I fixed yummy meals for the family when I had time and used purees anytime I was busy. I also stopped worrying about whether my child was meeting all her nutritional and iron requirements because I knew exactly how much of certain purees she consumed. I felt good about the fact that baby-led weaning gave my daughter the freedom to feed herself, but purees allowed me to wean her without driving myself crazy.

I started sharing this with other baby-led weaning moms and successfully showed them how to combine purees with solid foods. Parents expressed how it gave them peace of mind about meeting nutritional requirements, and they loved the flexibility. I also saw how some parents who were reluctant to try baby-led weaning were happier to attempt this combined method.

I found what worked for me and my baby, but something different might work for you. Whatever that method might be, I want to help you cut through all the nonsense and support your family throughout the weaning period.

Weaning is about exposing your child to as many foods as possible and allowing them to choose what to eat. As long as you understand your role and your baby's role in the weaning process, you can successfully feed purees or solid foods and still raise adventurous eaters with healthy eating habits.

Whether you have some knowledge of baby-led weaning, have never heard of it before, or you're looking for a fun and stress-free way to wean your baby, this book is for you. As we move forward, we will find the best, most balanced approach. I encourage you to be open-minded regardless of what you have read or heard. Different babies respond to different methods, and the key lies in figuring out what works for you and your little one. Remember, there is no one-size-fits-all.

I will cover everything you need to know about the weaning process so that you have the confidence and knowledge to execute whatever plan you choose. My goal is to prepare you for every situation you might face so that you can remain calm, in charge, and relaxed throughout.

Getting to this point took a lot of trial and error, and I've included everything I have learned along the way. For a busy working mom of four who is eager to give baby-led weaning a try, I've included:

- Easy batch prep strategies
- Three-ingredient recipes
- Foods you can buy in the grocery store that require little to no prep
- Quick strategies to adapt any adult meal and make it baby-approved

For the parent wanting to incorporate more spoon-feeding, I will share with you exactly how to take spoon-feeding to the next level and use it as a tool to enhance your child's experience around food.

This will be your one-stop guide on how to easily prepare meals, prevent picky eating, and enjoy the process. When you are thriving in parenthood, it sets your baby up for success, and a happy baby can be the source of boundless joy. So, are you ready to get going? Take a deep breath, put your baby in the driver's seat, and get ready for this fun and exciting journey.

Note: Solid food is usually defined as any solid substance (as opposed to liquid) used as a source of nourishment. Although solid food technically includes purees, for this book, I use the word solid to refer to whole foods served for baby-led weaning. When I use the word puree, I am referring to spoon-feeding.

Chapter 1

What in the World Is Baby-Led Weaning?

Weaning has taken on a lot of different forms over the 300,000 years that humans have been on Earth. Although the time and approach for weaning a child have changed over time, every civilization has successfully transitioned infants from breast milk to solid food, regardless of the means.

Weaning is the period in a child's growth when they are slowly transitioned to solid foods in place of breast milk or infant formula.[1] This time marks an important milestone in early development, and today it usually occurs around four to six months of age. Food preferences and eating behaviors will start to form, and these preferences can influence childhood and adult health and weight patterns. Whether this is your first time weaning or you have done it before, it is an important phase in the life of your little one, and you want to make sure you are setting your child up for success.

In most countries today, infants are introduced to solids through small amounts of spoon-feeding. However, recently, another way has evolved. It is infant-led self-feeding, known as baby-led weaning.

While I will focus on teaching you everything about baby-led weaning in the upcoming chapters, it's important first to discover how and why weaning has evolved over the ages, regardless of how fascinating or horrifying it might be.

1

The History of Weaning

Before the ages of Vitamix and food processors, our ancestors had to find other ways to prepare food suitable for a weaning baby. Hunter/gatherers, like other mammals, had learned to acquire food by hunting, fishing, and foraging for survival. With fewer resources than modern man, they offered their babies mashed-up fish and meat anywhere between their first and second birthdays.[2] Through each season, with the availability of different resources, what they fed their infants changed.

When the hunter/gatherers slowly became agriculturists in the Neolithic age, animal milk from sheep, cows, goats, and pigs became the perfect supplementary food for weaning. Milk was quickly adopted and considered highly nutritious to the point that wet nurses were only required to feed the baby for up to six months from birth. At this point, babies would be given cow's milk for another 18 months.[3]

Animal milk was not the only food that made its introduction into weaning during the Neolithic age. With agriculture booming, cereal porridge and bread became further commonly recommended foods. The addition of cow's milk and grains allowed mothers who had a poor milk supply to provide their babies with enough nutrition and calories to survive. In turn, the human population grew significantly.[4]

In fact, the addition of these two foods in the weaning process has had a profound and revolutionary effect on all walks of life. Even today, milk and flour are used in almost all cultures and ethnic groups during weaning, and serve as a staple in most adult diets. So, that covers the kinds of foods that have been commonly used in weaning – but what about the time period?

Although humans have used the same weaning foods throughout history, including grains, milk, fruit, and vegetables, the period of time after which we begin weaning our babies has changed dramatically.

Modern-day mothers are taught that there is a very specific time period after which you need to wean your baby. Parents are shamed if they wean their baby a little too early, or they worry that their child is developmentally behind if they wait too long. However, this has not always been the case, and going back to ancient and medieval times, things were very different.

The ancient world let babies live on breast milk for an exceptionally long time compared to the modern Western world. Greeks would wait twelve to eighteen months before weaning their babies, while the Romans and ancient Hebrews would wait until three years old – around the same time a baby's teeth came through.[5]

Medieval times were similar, and weaning could take place anytime from one to three years of age. Unlike the poor women, the rich would outsource the job of breastfeeding to wet nurses. When it was time to start weaning, the wet nurses would chew the food before giving it to the baby.[6] Of course, this was not hygienic and often introduced diseases to the children. Infant mortality skyrocketed.

From medieval times to the 16th century, things changed a lot. Babies began to be weaned much earlier than they had been before. Weaning took place anywhere between seven and nine months and babies were given supplementary breastfeeds until about 18 months old.[7] This practice is almost the same as it is today, but there were more changes in between.

By the 18th century, people became more fashion-conscious. Processed baby foods called "pap" were fed to babies as young as two months old! Pap was made from unpasteurized milk mixed with cereal and sometimes raw meat juices. During this time, it was common for a baby to be fully weaned by eight months old.[8]

When the 19th century rolled around, powdered infant milk was packaged in sterile containers, and this dramatically reduced infection rates in infants. Doctors started recommending that babies be weaned at one year of age, with pap and powdered milk.[9]

Unfortunately, by 1950, weaning took a turn for the worse. The general consensus was that breast milk did not contain enough essential vitamins, including iron, which led to solid foods being introduced even earlier. One 1953 weaning schedule recommended that babies be given solid food as early as two to three days.[10] Yes, two to three days after birth!

Luckily, things improved in the 1970s, and the Boomer generation was weaned starting at three months old.[11] Over the last 40 years, studies have shown that babies who are weaned later are much healthier, and thus, the standard weaning age became four to six months. Now, the World Health Organization recommends babies be breastfed entirely until six months of age.[12]

The Invention of Baby Food

According to Amy Bentley, in her book *Inventing Baby Food*, the widely known jars of baby food consisting of sweet potato and green peas didn't exist until the 1920s. When Harold Clapp's baby was sick due to his wife not being able to provide adequate breast milk, he made a soup from beef broth, vegetables, and cereal. Encouraged by how well his baby recovered and then thrived on these soups, he started making large batches of his mix and sold them to other parents through local pharmacies.[13]

The large food company Gerber also jumped on the wagon in 1920, when they transitioned their fruit and vegetable canning company into making purees labeled as "baby food."[14] With this began the first commercially available baby food on the market, and mothers quickly became intrigued.

As baby food started being mass-produced, it became an affordable option for most parents, and felt like the modern way to do things. Ad campaigns for baby food companies advertised that their canned and factory-made food was healthier than a mother's own homemade food, and parents felt guilty for using any other option.[15] Store-bought baby food was easier, sterile, and gradually, all new parents turned to it.

The baby food industry continues to thrive today by expanding its products into pouches, jars, and finger foods, but it is not the only way parents choose to wean their children in the 21st century.

The Term Baby-Led Weaning

In 2005, Gill Rapley was the first to coin the term baby-led weaning, or BLW. She concluded in her master's work in 2003 that six-month-olds have the necessary motor skills to feed themselves pieces of food.[16] This practice initially became popular in the United Kingdom and New Zealand, and it is now spreading to the rest of the world. Many practitioners prefer to call it baby-led feeding or auto-weaning, but at its core, it's a fancy name for finger food.

As parents ditch the spoons and put their children in control, they quickly realize how easy it is to allow the infant to choose for themselves how much and how quickly to eat. This is the case right from the age complementary food is usually introduced.

Rapley wanted parents to realize that infants are an active part of the feeding ladder and not just passive recipients.[17] To achieve this, foods the size of the baby's fist are offered as part of family meals, and they get to decide on everything else. It puts babies in a position where they are required to learn how to eat solid food, rather than passively swallowing purees. Instead of various foods being mixed and mashed together, food is served separately, giving the child freedom to eat whatever they want. Your only job as a parent is to respond to their cues and readiness.

More and more parents are moving away from purees and accepting baby-led weaning as their primary weaning method. On the other hand, the quick adoption has caused concern among some pediatricians and parents due to questions about adequate iron intake, other nutrient intake, and the risk of choking. Luckily, this concern has encouraged researchers and scientists to conduct studies that answer these questions.

Let's take a look at why BLW has been so quickly adopted and what the science says.

Benefits of the Baby-Led Weaning Method

Every parent has a different reason for doing BLW. Some parents simply prefer to feed their children scraps of food from their own plates.

Other parents fall in love with the notion that BLW will help them raise healthier and more developmentally advanced children. Regardless of your motives, there are so many phenomenal benefits your child receives when they have the freedom to control their own eating habits.

Lower Risk of Obesity

With a quick Google search, you will see parents worldwide jumping on the baby-led weaning train in hopes of lowering obesity rates in the long-term. Since food is placed in front of the child and not passively spooned into their mouth, they can self-regulate their food intake, and the risk of overfeeding is small.

Various studies have looked at how different weaning methods affect food preferences and BMI. In a 2012 study titled "Baby Knows Best?" researchers concluded that infants weaned through the baby-led approach are more likely to regulate their food and thus have a lower BMI index. They also noted that they had a preference for carbohydrates over sweets.[18]

In 2013, another study found similar results and noted: "Infants weaned using a baby-led approach were significantly more satiety-responsive and less likely to be overweight compared with those weaned using a standard approach."[19]

As adults, most of us are trying to figure out how to be intuitive eaters, but baby-led weaning allows your child to develop awareness right from the start. It empowers them to notice their hunger and satiety cues, so they learn to eat when hungry and stop when full.

The fact that you reach for that bag of potato chips when you're bored or that box of cookies when you're sad is not a coincidence. These habits are developed from the moment we start experimenting with food.

Adventurous and Less Picky with Food

We have all heard the stories from our parents about them making mac and cheese and broccoli for three months straight because it was the only thing we would eat. The real question is, was it just a phase, or was it a consequence of the way we were weaned?

When a child follows a baby-led weaning approach, they are able to explore different tastes, textures, aromas, and colors. A 2018 study concluded that a BLW approach increases dietary variety because of exposure to more textured foods at a young age. The children in the study also tended to eat more fruits and vegetables by the age of two than babies weaned on traditional purees.[20]

Picky eating has become one of the most common nutrition struggles most parents of toddlers face. Although most infants are fantastic eaters, they can suddenly refuse particular foods as they get older. This behavior is quite common and can be linked to a desire to gain independence, but it can also be caused by a parent pressuring the child to eat certain foods at a young age. If children feel forced to eat something, they are unlikely to enjoy it, and might start to reject all new foods outright because of a sense of fear and lack of control.

When children are purely spoon-fed, they don't have the independence to decide whether they are going to eat a particular food. BLW allows infants to decide when to try a new food, making it a positive, curious experience, rather than a negative one. In time, children are more willing to accept new foods as long as they know they don't have to eat something if they don't like it. Eventually, they learn to eat (almost) everything.

Improved Hand-Eye Coordination

As adults, we take for granted the skills required to transfer food from a plate into our mouths. However, for a baby, learning how to eat is hard and takes a lot of practice. A baby has to maintain eye contact with the food, decide to grab it with their fingers, successfully guide their hand to the food and bring it into their mouth multiple times a meal, and at least three times a day. BLW provides the perfect environment to practice these skills and foster a high level of motor skills from a young age.

Improved Dexterity

Picking up objects is another aspect that adults take for granted. Learning how to hold a piece of food without crushing it, pick up smaller pieces with just the thumb and forefinger, and use utensils are all advanced skills that need practice.

With several foods laid out in front of a child during baby-led weaning, they are constantly challenging their fine motor skills on many different shapes, sizes, and textures. The more practice a child is given, the faster their hand control develops. This leads into other skills and may help a child learn how to tie their shoes, catch a thrown object, or play a musical instrument.

Dental Benefits

Believe it or not, how your child's jaw develops at a young age determines whether they will need braces in the future or not. With baby-led weaning, babies are able to chew on solid foods, which encourages healthy jaw development. This movement expands the jaw to make room for all of their adult teeth and a fully open airway. Nutrition and genetics will also play a role in how the mouth develops, but chewing is one of the easiest ways to encourage healthy facial development.[21]

Improved Oral-Motor Skills

While chewing, swallowing, and tongue control can be observed in both puree-raised and baby-led-raised children, those who've experienced baby-led weaning appear to learn these skills much faster. Many parents report a reduction in gagging and choking during toddlerhood because their babies have so much practice using their mouths and tongues with real food from a young age.[22]

Activates the Five Senses

Spoon-feeding has become very popular over the last few decades, partly because of how mess-free it can be. When babies have the opportunity to explore food, they get it all over their hands, hair, clothes, and face. Spoon-feeding contains the mess to the bib and the baby's face, but this is not a very engaging experience for them.

Although it's not enjoyable to clean up multiple times a day, baby-led weaning activates all their senses. An infant has the opportunity to immerse itself in its food and learn how each food looks, smells, tastes, feels, and sounds while they eat.[23] This helps them learn and explore the world.

Confidence and Independence

When a baby is born, they spend months utterly incapable of doing anything for themselves. The confidence and independence that come with being able to feed themselves for the first time is unparalleled. With every food that they successfully pick up, bite, and swallow, they will realize that they can nourish themselves and do something independently.

After spending six months being waited on hand and foot, this is one of the first things that your baby will be able to learn to do on their own. Once your baby gets the hang of it, you will notice an instant boost of self-esteem that reflects on other aspects of life as they grow up.

Encourages Family Meals

Food is an integral part of our lifestyle and community. Although most families struggle to sit down at the dinner table together every night, baby-led weaning encourages this from the beginning.

In 2015, B. Morison and her colleagues published a paper comparing BLW to conventional, complementary feeding. They found that BLW promoted an early integration into family meals and that family meals happened more regularly.[24] Research also shows that children who participate in family dinners at least three times per week eat healthier foods, are less likely to have an eating disorder, have fewer problems at school, and have a better relationship with their parents.[25] Getting into the habit of eating together right from the start allows your baby to feel involved and develop social skills to communicate better.

Eat Fewer Processed Foods

Everywhere we turn, we are bombarded by processed foods. There is a fast-food restaurant on every block, and over 50 percent of the grocery store is full of processed snacks and meals. A BLW approach ensures that you ditch the highly processed foods and stick to fresh, nutrient-dense foods that can help your baby grow and develop. Research shows that exposing children to whole foods at a young age helps them to enjoy better nutrition in the long-term because they grow to love whole foods right from the start.

It's Fun!

Following a baby-led weaning approach is like playtime when an infant has the freedom to do whatever they want with the food. Exploring new textures, shapes, and sizes of food is very similar to playing with toys. Parents can also have fun experimenting with different foods and cooking new things.

Easier and Cheaper

If you are looking for something affordable, baby-led weaning can be much more budget-friendly than expensive store-bought cereals and purees. You also won't need to spend extra time mashing and mixing food and trying to make homemade purees. Most of the foods you already make for yourself can be slightly modified to make them safe for your child's age and abilities. If baby-led weaning is done right, it can easily save you money and time.

Of course, while the benefits of BLW are outstanding, you might find it interesting to read about some of the arguments against it, so you can weigh the merits for yourself.

The Fear of Choking

In all honesty, this question should have been in your head from the moment you read that baby-led weaning involves feeding children whole foods. I remember thinking to myself, *How in the world can I expect an infant to swallow solid food without choking?*

While your fears aren't misplaced, most people don't realize that choking and gagging are two very different things. Choking can be avoided if foods are correctly prepared, while gagging is a normal reflex that can happen with spoon-feeding or solids. Babies are born with a gag reflex to help them safely express foods that are too tricky for them to consume.

Numerous studies have been done to discover if parents are increasing the likelihood of their child choking with baby-led weaning. In 2016, one study concluded that "infants following a baby-led approach to feeding that includes advice on minimizing choking risk do not appear more likely to choke than infants following more traditional feeding practices."[26] It highlighted that choking episodes were due to a lack of education and advice on how to minimize the choking risk. Although promising, more research still needed to be done.

Two years later, the *Journal of the American Academy of Pediatrics* released a study involving 1,151 infants and showed that at least one episode of choking had occurred in both 11.9 percent of the strictly BLW group and 11.6 percent of the traditional weaning group. The scientists concluded that "baby-led weaning was not associated with an increased risk of choking."[27] In fact, they found that a baby-led approach gives the child more practice so they can learn how to be successful eaters.

Today, research continues to show that baby-led weaning carries no greater risk of choking than spoon-feeding and should not be a reason to avoid solids during weaning. Regardless of what method you use to wean your baby, it is always advised to take an infant first aid class to be prepared for any incident.

Nutrition Concerns

Other apprehensions quickly arose in the community as parents watched their infants barely consume any foods for the first few weeks to months. Were babies who followed a strict BLW approach going to be underweight? Would they be able to maintain adequate iron, zinc, and vitamin B12 levels?

In B. Morison's research done in 2015, she concluded that babies consumed the same amount of calories regardless of whether they were fed finger foods or purees. However, they also found that BLW babies consumed a higher intake of fat but a lower intake of iron, zinc, and vitamin B12.[28] Questions still remained on the absorption rate of the iron and whether the baby-led weaning infants were deficient in iron, because bloodwork was never done.

Three years later, a randomized control study out of Turkey concluded: "BLW can be an alternative complementary feeding type without increasing the risk of iron deficiency, choking, or growth impairment."[29]

Although breast milk or formula will provide almost all of the nutrients your baby needs until they are a year old, the nutrition a baby gets from baby-led weaning depends primarily on what you are offering. Parents who choose a BLW approach need to focus on providing foods that are appropriate for their child's skill level and are high in iron, protein, fat, vitamins, and minerals.

We have now uncovered the benefits of baby-led weaning and debunked some of the misconceptions about it, but is it right for every family and baby? Not necessarily.

Contraindications

Babies 4-6 Months

As appealing as BLW might sound, your doctor may recommend starting solid food as early as 17 weeks for constipation, acid reflux, allergy prevention, or other health concerns. It is unlikely that your baby will have developed the proper hand-to-eye coordination to successfully use this method and thrive at such a young age. In this instance, spoon-feeding is the best option, and you can always adopt a baby-led weaning approach later.

Premature Babies

Some premature babies have a more challenging time learning motor skills and can have developmental delays. Your child might not have the necessary skills to interact with food at six months or might not be able to sit up unassisted. It is also common for premature babies to show no interest in solid food when it is placed in front of them.[30]

In this instance, you do not want to wait until these skills develop. After your child has reached six months, they need to be getting some nutrients from other sources than breast milk and formula. Purees can be the best way to provide these. It is important to start your child on purees when your doctor recommends. It is likely that they still can follow a BLW approach later; it just might take a little longer for them to be ready.

Other

Baby-led weaning is also not recommended to babies with any genetic or neurological disorder, including developmental delays, hypotonia, or oral hypotonia. It is also not advised for babies at risk of dysphagia, including babies with anatomic disorders such as a cleft palate or tongue-tie.[31] For such babies, please consult your doctor; it is likely best to spoon-feed them for as long as possible.

BLW can help babies with Down syndrome, cerebral palsy, and other physical abnormalities by building core strength and improving hand movement. However, it is best to get a doctor's approval because these babies often have difficulties with swallowing early on and may need their diet supplemented with purees initially.[32]

Baby-led weaning might not be the best option for all babies at all times. Knowing what is suitable for your child is an essential aspect of parenthood and should not be neglected.

Luckily, if you don't think BLW is right for you, we can still incorporate its principles into spoon-feeding and receive similar benefits. On the other hand, if you are eager to start baby-led weaning but don't know if you can handle it, there are easy ways to make it less time-consuming, more rewarding, and stress-free. I will be covering all of this and more in the upcoming chapters.

Stay tuned!

Chapter 2
Eliminate the Rules!

While you may receive suggestions from many sides regarding weaning, a combination of spoon-feeding and BLW can be an ideal approach for most families. Why? Let me explain.

The baby-led weaning approach aims to encourage infants to learn how to self-feed instead of parents spooning the food into a passive baby's mouth. When an infant is able to self-feed, it removes any chance of force-feeding or pressure being exerted on the infant by the parent. BLW also allows the infant more opportunity to explore food combinations, tastes, and textures.

Although this all sounds rosy, it's not always realistic. Will you have time to feed your child a BLW meal three times a day? Will a daycare or your babysitter be willing to use this method? Will your baby get all their iron requirements?

Only you can answer these questions, but believe me, having the flexibility to offer both purees and solid food will make your life a whole lot easier.

When we combine both methods, we expose the baby to finger food, use purees as a tool to minimize any risk of nutritional gaps, and remove any pressure to conform to one weaning style. As such, mealtimes become easy, simple, fun, and enjoyable.

There is never a one-size-fits-all answer with parenting. Every baby is different, and your ability to adapt makes you a successful parent. Whenever you feed a baby, your primary focus should be on responding to their hunger and satiety cues and allowing them to decide when and how much to eat. These principles can be used whether you choose to spoon-feed, offer solid foods, or use a combination of both methods.

The Infamous 'Rules'

There are many online communities in the form of Facebook groups and blogs that offer a space to share experiences or tips. There are plenty aimed at parents who are BLW supporters.

Unfortunately, in many of these groups, moms shame other moms, preaching strict adherence to baby-led weaning and discourage all pureed food. Many parents feel pressured to do BLW, and doubt their parenting skills if they don't. Sometimes, the advice suggested on these platforms is misleading.

Moreover, some blogs expect strict obedience to the "rules" around BLW. I often see people in the groups claiming that these rules must be followed or your baby will not succeed. This can be a trigger for a lot of parents and discourages them from giving it a try. Frequently, the opinions and suggestions on these groups are often nothing more than common misconceptions and don't make sense in reality.

My two cents: Do not believe everything you read online.

The most common "rule" suggested by these online community sites or die-hard baby-led weaning parents is to "never combine traditional feeding (purees) with baby-led weaning (solids)." The most common reason stated for this is that baby-led weaning teaches babies how to chew first, and puree feeding teaches them how to swallow first. People fear that it will confuse the baby if you constantly switch between the two textures.

Another common "rule" is the suggestion that you should stop feeding purees for two weeks before starting baby-led weaning if your baby has already begun purees. This "rule" also suggests that applesauce and yogurt are the only purees "allowed" in a baby-led weaning. Furthermore, it says that purees are unnecessary, and parents should exclude them from baby diets because they have no benefits.

Why These "Rules" Make No Sense

Despite the prevalence of these strict "rules," many of them are not research-backed, and I'm entirely against half-cooked information. Babies learn how to swallow long before eating purees – by drinking breast milk and/or formula.

Since purees are just thickened liquid, if your baby knows how to swallow breast milk or formula, then they know how to swallow purees. Therefore, feeding your baby purees is not going to affect BLW any more than breastfeeding or bottle-feeding.[1] There is also no research that suggests that doing a combination of finger food and purees increases choking risk.[2] Additionally, yogurt and applesauce are the same as any other processed or homemade pureed food.

Purees do not negatively affect your weaning efforts. Parents should use them as a tool for nutrition when solid food is not feasible or to offer more variety. Parents should not be scared of them. Purees certainly do not speed up the weaning process, but they don't slow it down, either.

Since eating purees and solid food are two very different skills, it does not take your baby the magical number of two weeks to forget how to do one so that they can focus on the other. They constantly switch between these two skills every time they swap from breast milk/formula to solid food.

One piece of advice that may be useful is to avoid mixing purees and solids in a single dish of food. Sorting solid chunks of food from a liquid is an advanced skill that takes time to learn. Soup is an excellent example of one of these trickier foods. Some babies might ignore the chunks in the liquid if they are small enough and swallow them without chewing, but it is still best to avoid these types of foods when your baby starts weaning.[3]

Keeping these facts in mind, ignore the common online judgment, and use your own critical thinking skills. Baby-led weaning should be fun. Luckily, we can easily remove the rules, fear, and stress by combining these two weaning methods when needed.

Benefits of Adding Spoon-Feeding to Baby-Led Weaning

Although it is not necessary to combine spoon-feeding with BLW, there are benefits for your baby and it can take a lot of the pressure off you. Below are some of the benefits of using purees alongside baby-led weaning.

1. Introduce Potential Allergens at an Earlier Age

Every year, food allergies become more common among infants. Although it's not something that we usually think about when it comes to weaning, it is good to be aware of how to decrease the risk of your child becoming allergic to common foods.

Based on the most recent data, it is recommended that you introduce allergenic foods at four to six months of age.[4] The earlier these foods are introduced into a child's life (with regular exposure), the less likely the child is to develop allergies. It is unlikely that your child will be ready for BLW at four months old, but if you have a history of allergies, you can use purees to test allergies as early as four months.

2. Assure Adequate Nutrition

Although a well-balanced solid food diet during BLW can provide all the required nutrients, there is still a lot of debate on the topic, and some parents might choose to supplement with purees. Some parents may also struggle to find enough time to prepare fresh meat and other sources of iron during baby-led weaning.

Iron-rich purees can be an excellent addition to any weaning diet and can be bought in the supermarket or made at home by blending liver, meat, and other iron-rich foods. Baby cereal and baby oats fortified with extra iron can also be purchased in the baby food aisle.

Some parents might also worry if their child is underweight or experiencing developmental delays, and is still not able to eat much food by the time they are nine to ten months old. Purees are a fantastic way to add extra calories and nutrients to encourage weight gain and meet nutritional requirements. Mashing or blending any food with sour cream, coconut oil, butter, avocado, or other additions can provide extra calories.

3. Variety of Texture and Tastes

While you are weaning your baby, you want to expose them to as many different foods as possible.[5] Adding purees to your baby's diet is a great way to expose them to foods that are too challenging or a potential choking risk when whole. You can even offer the same food to your baby but in two different ways – one in solid form and one mashed. This provides the same taste, with two different textures.

If there is a food your child has previously rejected in its whole form, it may be worth mashing or pureeing it and offering it on a spoon. You might be surprised by how some infants will eat foods with the same taste but a different texture. You can also mix various food into one puree and hide the taste of food that your child has so far disliked.

4. Flexibility

Choosing a combined diet of both pureed and solid foods gives you flexibility and more options while feeding your baby at home or on the go. Life is sometimes hectic and you might find that you and your baby enjoy spoon-feeding every once in a while. A combination allows you to adapt to your baby's mood and pick whatever will work best at that particular time instead of always relying on one form of food.[6] Purees can also be a lifesaver if you are out with your baby and can't do BLW.

Each Baby Is Different

Every baby and family has its own needs, and there are no set rules that work best for everyone. Here are some things to consider:

- Find out your baby's interests, skills, and abilities and decide what options are best for your baby. Most children thrive with a combination of the two.

- Just because one baby did great on baby-led weaning doesn't mean all others will do too. Each baby thrives on something different.
- Your baby might be fussy and more inclined to try purees at first because of their similarity to breast milk.
- Your baby may simply not be interested in solid foods, and it's perfectly okay to delay introducing solids and start with purees.
- Some babies might instantly respond well to solid foods. In such a case, you don't ever need to spoon-feed, but you can occasionally add purees for a variety of textures.

There are massive benefits to your child's growth and development when you offer solid foods, but is baby-led weaning right for you as a parent? There are a lot of factors that you need to consider before deciding if you will thrive with this weaning method.

Each Parent Is Different

Just as every baby has its own needs and differs from all other babies, so does each parent. Not all parents react to challenges in the same way. You need to consider how each type of feeding method affects you as a parent as well. To get a better idea of this, ask yourself these questions:

Are you okay with a mess?

If you give utmost importance to cleanliness, you should know that your baby will find it difficult to differentiate between eating and playing. Food will likely be all over the floor, highchair, and baby after every meal. The bottom line is, you need to be okay with your baby making a mess before you commit to this approach.

Do you have the time?

On average, it takes about 30-45 minutes from start to finish for a baby-led weaning meal. If you do this three times a day, you will be spending a lot of your time watching your baby eat and cleaning up after them. Incorporating this into family meals can make it less time-consuming, and there are ways to make the cleanup process smoother, but it is still a commitment. In the beginning, you need to be able to offer uninterrupted time. However, as your confidence improves and your baby becomes more proficient with eating, it will get easier.

Can you have patience?

Learning to eat solid foods can be more challenging than you might think. It is a very slow process, and you must give your baby the space and time to learn on their own. Remember, your baby gets to decide how quickly or slowly they want to eat. They have complete control over the meal. Although you might start offering your child solid food at six months, you should know that they might not start ingesting anything until around eight or nine months. On top of that, you might be spending most of the time just watching them play with the food. Patience goes a long way in helping your baby develop the necessary skills to eat.

Are you able to remain calm when your baby gags?

Everyone has different emotional responses to things around them. You may react more impulsively than other parents may, and in such cases, baby-led weaning might prove too stressful for you. Babies will undoubtedly gag even during spoon-feeding, but it can be harder not to panic when they are eating solids.

This question is critical because babies do not think that gagging is a big deal. Air can still flow into their lungs, so it doesn't scare them unless they see their caregiver freaking out. You need to stay calm as you watch your baby cough and expel the challenging food. Getting your baby worked up will cause more harm than good.

Are you going to second-guess yourself?

This is the most common thing that I see with parents who have committed to baby-led weaning. They second-guess every food they prepare and worry about the correct size, shape and nutrients of every single meal.

Constantly feeling stressed and worrying that you are doing everything wrong is not the right way to approach baby-led weaning. Confidence will come with time, but there are simple guidelines I will outline over the next few chapters, so you never have to worry about whether you are doing it right.

The Most Important Thing When It Comes to Feeding

Purees are not the devil, but how we feed purees can be a real issue. Luckily, we can easily improve the way we spoon-feed to enjoy some of the benefits offered by BLW if we focus on what is important about feeding.

The most meaningful way of feeding a baby – regardless of method or diet – is to follow a "responsive feeding" approach. Responsive feeding means you adjust your feeding habits according to your baby's needs, eliminating all pressure.[7] BLW principles are all about building a healthy relationship with food and giving the baby control.

Acknowledging your baby's needs will create a healthy eating environment and teach your baby skills for self-regulation and self-control. Responsive feeding has several benefits in that it allows the baby to develop and recognize its own hunger cues and fullness cues. It can also help prevent feeding aversions, because babies control what goes in their mouths and, in turn, they begin to look forward to meals.

It is also essential to have a clear division of responsibilities. As a parent, your job is to decide when, where, and what to feed. Your child decides whether to eat at all and how much to eat.[8] By knowing and keeping your responsibilities separate, you can have a stress-free weaning experience. So, how do we adapt spoon-feeding to let your baby call the shots? We will explore this next.

How to Improve Spoon-Feeding

Baby-led spoon-feeding can seem foreign if you have no experience. Also, if your baby is new to it, it could take up to 30 minutes or so for one meal. This is because the baby has control over what goes into their mouths and leads the process. The easiest way to improve spoon-feeding for your baby is by trusting them.

Any spoon-feeding should be offered separately from solid food. Refrain from feeding purees after a baby-led weaning meal as a way to fill up the child. In this instance, it would discourage the child from learning how to eat solid food on their own because purees would always be there afterward.

Here are some general introductory instructions for your first baby-led spoon-feeding meal.[9]

Step 1: Introduce purees when your baby is developmentally ready, i.e. sits up unassisted, has good head control, etc. (more extensively covered in Chapter 3). If your child is under six months of age, ensure spoons have been sterilized.

Step 2: Place your baby sitting upright in a stable position. You want the baby to feel safe and comfortable while eating.

Step 3: Offer the baby a taste of the food by placing a small amount on a pacifier or finger before offering the spoon (optional).

Step 4: Hold the spoon six to twelve inches (15-30 cm) from the child's face with roughly ½ teaspoon of a runny liquid puree.

Step 5: Observe your baby's reaction.

Possible reactions:

- If the child opens their mouth, try placing the spoon on the child's bottom lip and let the child suck the puree off the spoon.
- If the child also moves their head toward or reaches for the spoon, guide the spoon toward the back corners of the mouth or middle of the tongue. Wait for the baby to close its lips. You can gently press down onto the tongue with the spoon to trigger the lips to close. Next, wait for the child to remove the contents off the spoon or slowly remove the spoon straight back out. Refrain from tilting it upwards at an angle.
- If your child does nothing or starts fussing, don't force it. Put the spoon away and repeat another time or day.

Step 6: If you notice that your child's response is good, you should continue to feed with small bites at a slow pace.

By following this approach, you slowly teach your baby that the puree they are eating fills them up and relieves hunger. It can take a child a while to make the connection that food will satisfy them the same way formula or breast milk does. Although it might seem like a prolonged process, you are giving the baby time for their saliva to mix with the puree and enhance their digestion. This will also give them time to register whether they are full. If a baby eats too fast, they can easily overeat before their stomach tells their mind they have had enough.

More Advanced Options as the Baby's Skills Develop

As your baby has more practice with spoon-feeding, they will quickly be ready for an additional challenge. Weaning is your time to allow your baby to figure out how to eat everything on their own, so once they have mastered swallowing thin purees, give them additional skills to practice. Here are some more advanced options to consider as your baby's skills develop:

- Increase the amount of puree on the spoon.
- Increase the thickness of the puree and introduce foods that tend to stick to the spoon, like watered-down nut butter.
- You and your baby can hold the spoon together as you help guide the spoon into the baby's mouth.
- Pre-load the spoon and hand it to the baby to take and guide it toward their mouth.
- Feed one bite, then let the baby feed itself the next bite unassisted.
- Pre-load the spoon and then place it on a highchair for the baby to pick up and self-feed.

What Not to Do

We've seen spoon-feeding in movies from childhood, and it gives us an odd idea of what it is supposed to look like. A stressed-out mom quickly shovels food into a baby's mouth and wipes excess off their face after every bite. Although this is how Hollywood might do it, you want to be present and aware of every action you take as a parent to ensure the baby is in control. Here are some tips on what not to do when feeding a baby with a spoon.

- Remove sayings such as "here comes the airplane." Although it might put a smile on your little one's face, it is not a healthy approach to eating. Anything that tricks your baby into opening their mouth and accepting the spoon should be avoided.
- Avoid forcing food into your baby's mouth when they are distracted or not interested. Distracting your baby makes it difficult for them to tap into their satiety cues and increases their risk of overeating.
- Never remove the puree off the spoon by scraping it up against the baby's gums or lips. The child should remove the food by using their lips, tongue, and cheeks. Have some patience with this and never force your baby even if you don't get the desired results.
- Avoid mindlessly stuffing food into your baby's mouth. Be present when you feed your baby. A positive eating experience is built on awareness.
- Try to avoid placing the spoon deep inside the child's mouth when feeding to prevent unnecessary gagging or vomiting.
- Don't clean the food off the baby's mouth or bib until they are completely done eating. Babies need to get messy and touch food with their skin so they activate all their senses.[10]

Timeline

As you embrace your baby-led spoon-feeding journey, here are some rough guidelines on what to expect:[11]

- 6-9 months—The baby will need assistance from you with things like getting the spoon in their mouth, so make sure that this is a joint effort.
- 9 months—The baby should begin to hold a spoon completely on their own.

- 12-14 months—Child can easily bring a spoon with food on it to their mouth unassisted.

What a Combo Method Looks Like

There are many ways you can successfully combine spoons and solids to create a weaning method. Be flexible and do whatever works for you. There is never a wrong way to do it as long as you avoid foods like chunky soups. All of the combinations below are common and may give you some ideas about how it could work for you.

- Try baby-led weaning on weekends and weeknights. Spoon-feeding can be used during the day on weekdays when your schedule might be more hectic.
- Try baby-led weaning for breakfast and dinner and use spoon-feeding when you are out and about during the day.
- Try feeding your child the same food as you for dinner from time to time. For example, if you're cooking roasted veggies with salmon and mashed potatoes, your baby can eat the same thing. Simply prepare the foods in a BLW-approved shape and hold off on the salt and any other spicy seasoning.
- Stuck in a pinch at a friend's house or restaurant? You can easily take some appropriate foods from your own plate that your child can eat without advanced preparation or serving special food.
- Spoon-feeding can be used when your child is with a babysitter or at daycare. Nannies/babysitters unfamiliar with BLW may be more comfortable with spoon-feeding.
- If you're not preparing food for yourself and don't have anything already pre-made, you can easily supplement with purees.
- Offer a bowl of puree with a BLW meal so your baby can use their hands to scoop it up, or dip other foods into it. Purees don't have to be only offered on a spoon.
- If your child is a fussy eater and does not show any particular interest in solid food, it may help to focus on

purees for a few days or weeks and slowly warm them up to solids.
- Begin with purees for the first few weeks and slowly transition into BLW as your confidence grows.

There are a lot of options, and it's up to you to find out what works best for your family. Trial-and-error is your friend, and you cannot always figure out things in a single attempt. On top of that, your child will constantly be changing. Don't expect everything to go right on the first try. Give it some time and patience, and keep experimenting. There's no right or wrong, as long as the child gets fed!

Chapter 3
When and How to Get Ready

Despite popular belief, weaning can actually be relatively easy. Your success is directly related to starting at the right time. For the most part, as long as your child is developmentally ready for food, they will figure it out.

It is also important to be prepared and have a decent understanding of what to expect. Although things won't always go to plan, I want you to feel confident and ready for anything. I will address getting ready and some common safety concerns in this chapter.

Milk Is the Staple Diet

There is no other food better than breast milk or formula for a growing infant. Keep this in mind throughout your weaning journey; breast milk or formula should be your baby's primary source of nutrition until one year of age.[1]

During the first few weeks to months of weaning, how much food they consume will not be important. Instead, pay attention to how they become accustomed to the idea of eating food. The energy and nutrients they require to thrive will be gained from breast milk or formula, so continue to offer all feeding sessions.

When Is Your Baby Ready?

The American Academy of Pediatrics recommends breastfeeding or using formula exclusively until six months of age.[2] However, they acknowledge that most babies are ready to start weaning between four to six months old. Some studies also state that it is easier for children to accept complex flavors from four to six months old.[3]

As we have seen throughout history, our ancestors started weaning from as early as two days to as late as two years. It is safe to say that babies are very resilient and can adapt to whatever modern man decides to throw at them. Although infants will not have the necessary skills to pick up and bring solids to their mouths, they might be ready for purees as early as four months old. In most instances, start looking for signs that your baby is ready to wean at four months, but don't expect to see these until closer to six months of age.

Signs That Your Baby Is Ready for Purees

Each baby is different in many aspects. Their initial birth weight, genetics, metabolism rate, physical health, and growth milestones all play roles in deciding when it is right to start giving them purees. Your doctor might also recommend starting purees early for a variety of reasons. Below are signs that your infant is ready for semi-solid food, known more commonly as purees.

Losing the Tongue-Thrust Reflex

Babies have an innate "tongue thrusting" impulse that triggers the tongue to extend and stick out of the mouth. This can be stimulated by anything that touches the tongue and it can last anywhere from four to seven months of age. If this impulse is still present, it will swiftly push any item out of the mouth to help keep an infant's airway clear.[4] It will be difficult for them to hold anything in their mouth, let alone swallow purees, until they have lost this reflex.

Sitting up With Support

Your child must be able to sit up with support from a highchair. Although the highchair might help them stay in a seated position, they should have the control to hold up their head unassisted.[5] This is an important milestone as it shows that the baby's sensory and motor functions are ready for food.

Drawing up Lower Lip

During breastfeeding or formula feeding, babies primarily use their tongues to eat by sucking liquid directly into their throats. They don't need to use their lips to hold liquid in their mouths.

However, to eat food, their lips and tongues need to be able to hold food in their mouths for a few seconds before swallowing it. That means that when a baby draws in their lower lips (for example, as you take a spoon out of their mouth), they can successfully eat. Until this occurs, food will just fall right back out of the mouth, so look for signs that your infant can draw in their upper and lower lips.[6]

Showing Interest

You may notice your baby slowly start showing an interest in eating. They might watch you while you eat. This is a great indication that they are curious about trying the food.

Signs Your Baby Is Ready for Baby-Led Weaning

In order to start BLW, a child will need slightly more advanced motor skills and muscle strength compared to spoon-feeding. As Gill Ramsey pointed out in her master's work, babies typically develop these skills at six months of age and can successfully feed themselves pieces of food.

Age and Weight

The age and weight of your baby can give you a rough idea of whether it is ready for BLW, but of course, these are just guidelines, and there will always be exceptions. Babies will be developmentally ready at different times.

Six months is the typical age when most babies have hit the necessary milestones and are capable of starting to consume solid food. If your baby was born prematurely, it would be best to use their "corrected age" by taking your baby's age in weeks and subtracting the number of weeks your baby was preterm.[7]

Another indicator that doctors will use is if your baby has doubled its body weight since birth. When you look at growth charts, this generally occurs around six months old.[8] Some professionals use this indicator because it means the baby is growing well and hitting all the milestones. However, each baby grows differently, and not all babies who have hit these age and weight requirements are ready to eat solid food.

Physical Signs

When your baby starts to coordinate their eyes, hand, and mouth, it can be a great time to start solids. You want your child to be able to look at an item, pick it up, and put it in their mouth.[9] A lot of times, this sign can be seen when they are playing with toys. If a child is able to put a toy in their mouth, their coordination may be good enough for BLW.

You also want your child to be able to sit up with minimal support and be able to hold their head still.[10] If your child has to be propped up in a highchair, then it is unlikely that they will feel secure or interested in trying something new. If they can sit up alone, this gives them confidence and a sense of control.

If you have started feeding your child purees, ask yourself if they can move the food around in their mouth and swallow it instead of spitting it right out. If they can successfully do this, then this is another indicator that they are ready for solid food.

Note: Babies do not need teeth to eat solid food. Their gums are extremely strong and hard and can mash any soft food that you offer them.[11] As they begin teething and their molars and front teeth start to come in, they will be able to tackle harder and bigger pieces of food, but their gums can handle the basics initially.

Behavioral Signs

Regardless of how developmentally ready your child is for solid food, they need to have a desire to eat and try something new if they are going to succeed with baby-led weaning. If your child closely watches all your movements, makes noises, or reaches for the food you are eating, this shows they are curious about trying something new.[12]

Although it will still be challenging at first, your baby is telling you that they want to do what you are doing. Babies love to imitate their parents, and eating is no exception.

If you have been feeding your infant purees, it is important to point out that it is never too late to incorporate BLW, regardless of your child's age. All you need to do is start at a beginner level and offer recommended foods for six-month-olds first, regardless of the child's actual age.

Now that we have covered whether your child is ready for purees or solid food, let's go over what you need to know to make this a safe and effortless transition.

Choking vs. Gagging Basics

There is a lot of confusion among parents on what gagging and choking are, and they are often used interchangeably even though they are two very different reflexes.

The gag reflex is the reaction of coughing in order to spit out food that is too big or too hard to swallow. This reflex is set into motion when food touches a specific part of an infant's tongue because, unlike adults, babies do not have the proper mouth coordination to prevent themselves from choking.[13] A baby's gag reflex is rapid and sensitive as they learn to coordinate food around their mouth.

As your baby starts experimenting with food, anything too challenging for their current skill level will be coughed up and spat out. Around six months of age, your baby's gag reflex will likely be located near the middle of the tongue and it will be extremely sensitive to protect your child from choking.

As your child grows and experiments with more foods, this reflex will move toward the back of the throat and become less sensitive. This typically happens between seven and twelve months of age.[14]

The gag reflex will still be present to prevent choking, but it will be less sensitive.

Your baby should be able to successfully eat bigger and more challenging foods at this point, as long as they have had adequate practice. This is another step toward them gaining total control over their muscles.

Managing the patterns of chewing, swallowing, and breathing is complicated, so there will be times when your baby gags more often, and times when they seem like a champion eater. If your baby is gagging more frequently, it can mean that the foods they're trying to eat are too challenging or that they have learned to move food around in their mouths with their tongue.

You're probably wondering how you can avoid gagging altogether – but you probably can't. Although you can refrain from giving your child anything difficult to eat, this is how they learn. It is likely that anytime they are introduced to something new or different, they will gag.

Even new textures can be challenging and trigger the gag reflex, like transitioning from a liquid puree to a slightly thicker puree. However, it should give you peace of mind knowing that it is usually a short learning curve, and gagging decreases dramatically a few weeks after introducing solids.

The good news is that your infant can safely experiment with new foods and textures and practice picking things up with little fear of choking. The benefit of starting baby-led weaning early is that by the time the gag reflex moves to the back of the throat, your child's skills around eating will be relatively well developed.

Choking, on the other hand, occurs when the baby can neither swallow nor spit out a large chunk of food. As a result, the food will get stuck in their throat, and their body cannot expel it on its own. When a child is choking, the food is blocking their airflow and intervention is needed by an adult.[15] Although this is uncommon as long as you prepare and cut foods correctly, it is essential to keep a constant watch on your baby throughout the meal.

Signs of Gagging

Gagging is very obvious and noisy. If you imagine a choking child, this is probably an accurate representation of gagging. Your baby will be spluttering, coughing loudly, gurgling, and might even cry or fuss. Gagging can even cause the face to turn red and the eyes to water, but the baby can still breathe.[16] These are all just mechanisms to help the baby expel the challenging food.

What to Do When Your Child Is Gagging

Don't intervene. Although it might be hard to sit and watch, your child's body knows exactly how to remove the food, so it is safer if you do not intervene.[17] I know you will feel the urge to help your baby, but you might do more harm than good.

Signs of Choking

Unlike gagging, choking is very quiet. Once a portion of food is stuck in a baby's throat, it will be hard for them to breathe, make sounds, or cry for help. Their eyes will get watery, and in that awful state of not knowing what is happening, they will have a look of terror.[18]

If they continue choking, their skin may also turn to blue, to purple, to ash-like. They will likely have trouble coughing, and even though their mouth will be open, the tongue will not be thrust forward.[19]

What to Do When Your Baby Is Choking

Again, do not panic. You do not want the baby to feel more panicked than they already are. The most important thing to remember is never put your fingers in their mouth to try and remove the stuck food. Trying to remove the food with your fingers can lodge the food deeper into their throat and make matters worse.

The best way to help your baby while they are choking is with the physical action called the Heimlich maneuver. This is usually done on anyone who is choking, irrespective of their age and size.

Follow these steps to successfully perform the Heimlich maneuver on a choking baby:[20]

1. Place your baby facing down over your forearm in a seated position. Support their head with your non-dominant hand. Your baby's head should be lower than their midsection, so gravity is working in their favor.
2. With the heel of your dominant hand, give five blows that are forceful and rapid between your baby's shoulder blades.
3. If the food is still stuck, turn your baby over and give five chest thrusts with your index and middle finger in the middle of their breastbone (located just below the nipples). You should see their chest compressing 1/2 inch to 3/4 of an inch (between 1 and 2 cm).
4. Alternate between five back blows and five chest thrusts until the object becomes dislodged, and your baby can breathe on their own. At this point, it is safe to help remove the piece of food from their mouth if they haven't already got it out.

If the infant loses consciousness, perform CPR and call 911.

There is no easy way to say this. Watching your baby learn how to eat, whether it's purees or solid food, can be very scary. It is important to educate yourself so you can remain calm and relaxed during the entire weaning process. Take an infant first aid class if you haven't already. If you can educate yourself on what you should do if something goes wrong, you will be confident and in control of the moment.

If you are unfamiliar with the Heimlich maneuver or need more information on infant first aid, I have provided more resources and links to videos at the end of Chapter 10.

Preparation for Baby-Led Weaning

Moving on from the frightening side of things, let's talk about cleanup. BLW is messy, but there are some simple ways to make cleaning up quick and effective. There will be a lot of smashing, smearing, and dropping food during a BLW meal. Instead of spending half your day cleaning up your baby, the highchair, and your floor, buy products that will simplify the process.

A highchair will be one of your most used possessions during this time, so you can save yourself a lot of headaches by making sure it is easy to clean. If your highchair has any padding or cloth lining that cannot be easily wiped down, I highly recommend removing it. You want a highchair that can be wiped down after every meal, or you could easily spend 15-30 minutes just cleaning it.

Look for a highchair that has these characteristics:[21]

- It is the right height and shape so it can easily fit at your dinner table and allow your family to eat together. It helps if it is compact and light.
- It is comfortable and allows your baby to sit upright, with good posture.
- It comes with a footrest or has a footrest that can be attached. Proper foot support helps with core strength and allows your baby to sit upright for 30 minutes to an hour without getting tired.
- It is durable and will last until your child turns two. A lot of highchairs can grow with your child and be adapted into different shapes and sizes.
- It can be cleaned easily with a few wipes of a rag or towel. Avoid anything with nooks and crannies.
- It has a wide tray to reduce food falling on the ground.
- The tray is adjustable or at a height where the baby can comfortably reach the food.

You also want to invest in a good bib. Bibs have been used for decades to protect children from staining their clothes, but when it comes to baby-led weaning, you'll need a bib that can do it all. I recommend you invest in something that can easily be cleaned or put in the dishwasher. Bibs that cover your baby's arms and have a pocket to catch falling food can also assist with cleanup. If it's warm enough, your baby can eat in just a bib and a diaper. Skin is often easier to clean than fancy bibs.

Along with this, it is helpful if you can cover the ground around their highchair with something that can be cleaned or thrown away.

A garbage bag, shower curtain, plastic tablecloth or splat mat are all great options that are easy to remove and clean.

Lastly, buy a few plates and bowls that are designed for BLW. They should be easy to clean and have a built-in suction that will keep them in place as your baby removes the food.

Some people recommend that you forget about dishes and place all the food directly on your child's highchair tray. Although you are welcome to give this a try, it is difficult for a baby to pick things up from a flat surface with a minimal lip. Having BLW-appropriate dishes gives your baby an edge for the food to press up against instead of it sliding all around the highchair tray.

If your baby is under six months, you should sterilize all plates, bowls, or spoons. After six months, your child's digestive and immune systems will be more mature. At this point, wash dishes in hot soapy water or use the dishwasher.[22]

Go to www.thefirst12months.com/#bonusblw to see my most recent and up-to-date recommendations for all these items and more.

Preparation for Spoon-Feeding

Yes, even spoon-feeding needs preparation if it is done correctly. Getting the proper utensils to spoon-feed your baby is as important as getting the right food.

The shape and size of the spoon should match the child's mouth. You want to select a spoon that easily fits inside the baby's mouth and has a shallow bowl. This is especially important for beginners or any infant with delayed motor skills, because removing the puree from the spoon requires less effort.

It is also helpful to select an appropriate spoon handle. If your child has reached the point where they can self-feed a puree at least some of the time, it is best to have a child-size handle. If you want to alternate between self spoon-feeding and being fed by a caregiver, then have two spoons available – one with a long handle and one with a child-size handle.[23]

Spoon material is also something you want to be aware of. Stainless steel can be sturdy and easy for an adult to use, but it can be heavy and difficult for an infant to use on their own. Plastic or silicone spoons are lighter and can be more comfortable for a child, although they are not as durable.[24] Typically, a silicone or plastic spoon is best in the beginning, and as the baby's skills advance, you can transition to stainless steel.

Go to www.thefirst12months.com/#bonusblw to see my most recent and up-to-date recommendations for all these items and more.

How Often Should You Feed the Baby Purees/Solids?

Breast milk and formula will still be their primary food source, so start feeding purees or solid food once to twice a day to begin with. If your family sits down together every night, this is a great time to incorporate an infant meal. Over time, as your child's interest in food increases, gradually add more meals.

For the first few weeks, don't be too concerned with following a schedule or missing meals. There will be days when your baby doesn't feel like eating, and other days when you end up having three meals together. You can disregard any need for a meal to be eaten at a specific time or spaced out throughout the day. Simply try to eat with your baby as much as possible to provide a sense of community, and everything else will work itself out.

To make sure your baby is consuming enough breast milk or formula, it is usually best to offer solids or purees 45-90 minutes after a feed. This ensures that you're offering food when your baby isn't starving.[25] Although it seems like they are less likely to eat, this is beneficial because it is too frustrating to learn a new skill when hungry. Offering solids after a feed also guarantees that your baby is not full before a breast or bottle-feeding session. This will encourage the child to consume enough breast milk or formula to get the required nutrition.

Don't be concerned about offering too many meals in one day. As long as your baby is happy and having fun with food, there is no harm in doing three sessions in a day right from the beginning. Remember, it is unlikely that they are eating much, so view it as lots of practice and playtime. Every child will have a tolerance for how much they can handle in one day.

Below is a rough guide on how you should introduce solids/purees into your infant's diet. Alter this to suit you and your child.

- 4-6 months—1 meal per day
- 6-8 months—2 meals per day
- 8-12 months—3 meals per day
- 12 months plus—3 meals a day along with snacks.

Chapter 4
How to Prepare a Meal

Preparing your first foods for your baby can be both exciting and confusing. There will always be a learning curve with anything new you try, but with a few guidelines, you can quickly learn how to select the right food and prepare it properly. Remember, although the baby decides how much to eat, it is still your job to offer them a healthy variety of food and prepare it in the right way and to the right size.

While it might seem like a lot of time and thought has to go into what food to offer, how much to offer, and in what portion sizes, it can actually be relatively straightforward. The key is never to overcomplicate your infant's meals. In most situations, you can easily and quickly modify anything you are already making for yourself so it is appropriate for your baby. This will not only save you time and money, but it makes baby-led weaning almost easier than spoon-feeding. Let's walk through the preparation and serving of foods for BLW.

Quantity

Initially, you can begin by introducing one new food per meal. This makes it less overwhelming for the baby and gives them enough time to explore each food offered. As they gradually become more familiar with the foods, increase the number of food items provided to three to four per meal.

In the beginning, it is easier to offer foods separately so you can gauge your child's reaction to each ingredient. Over time, these foods can be combined into common foods like hummus on toast, spaghetti and meatballs, or pancakes. By keeping food separate in the beginning, you can also successfully identify any allergic reaction.

Size

Almost all babies will have developed a palmar grasp by the time they reach six months. This means that they can easily bring their fingers toward their palm and pick something up. On the other hand, the pincer grasp will not develop until around eight to nine months of age, so they will not be able to pick something up with just their thumb and forefinger.

Palmer Grasp

In order to accommodate their palmar grasp, foods need to be cut into long, thin strips so they can easily pick them up with their whole palm in the beginning.

A good rule is to cut food to the size of an adult's finger, or roughly 3-4 inches long, by 1/2 inch wide, by 1/2 inch deep (9 x 1.3 x 1.3 cm).[1] This will make it difficult for the baby to force the entire piece of food fully into their mouth (causing them to choke) but will ensure it is large and long enough to grab it with their fist. Ideally, you want the pieces big enough so a bit is sticking out when they hold it in their fists.

To scale food size and shape for 6-9 month old babies (palmer grasp)

There is not usually a risk of providing pieces of food that are too large. Choking occurs when the pieces are too small. It is therefore better to offer bigger pieces that don't fully fit in their mouth. Examples of big pieces could be half a slice of bread, half a banana, and a big slice of watermelon without seeds.

There is no way to completely eliminate the risk of your baby choking on portions of food, but there are many basic rules you can follow to minimize this risk.

- Cut everything you can into long, thin strips. Bigger is better than too small.
- Avoid cutting foods in a circle or round shape.
- Bendy foods like bread and pancakes can be cut slightly wider (the size of two adult fingers).
- If food cannot be cut into a long strip, think about other portioning methods. Broccoli or cauliflower, for example, can be cut into big florets.
- Steak and other meats should be cut against the grain into strips, so the meat is tender and doesn't break apart into small pieces.
- Avoid serving round and firm foods like grapes and cherry tomatoes.

- Slightly flatten or slice round fruits in half (like blueberries, raspberries, and other similar foods).
- Remove all pits and seeds.

Texture

You guessed it right. Almost everything should be soft – so soft that it can be easily mashed when gently pressed between your thumb and forefinger. That said, foods should not be mushy, or your baby will not be able to pick them up. Some foods that are not soft are still okay as long as they do not break into pieces. A great example of this is ribs or drumsticks.

It is also essential for your baby to be introduced to a variety of textures in their early months of weaning. Every texture will be a new challenge and hence it will improve their skills.

The following textures should be incorporated into your baby's diet:[2]

- Chewy: bread, meat, cookies, pasta, rice
- Sticky: nut butter
- Creamy: avocado, banana, yogurt, mashed potatoes
- Stringy: shredded beef, pineapple
- Rubbery: mushrooms, calamari, shrimp
- Spongy: tofu, eggs
- Juicy: pear, plum, mango
- Mushy: thick purees, apple sauce
- Runny: thin purees
- Firm: cheddar cheese
- Crunchy: cucumber, red peppers (if under one year, only for sucking on)

Try to expose your baby to as many tastes and textures as possible between six and twelve months of age as each will provide a unique challenge. A good goal is to introduce your baby to over 100 different foods by the time they reach their first birthday. If you start weaning at six months, you will have roughly 180 days until your baby turns one. If you only introduced a new food every other day, which should be generally doable; that's already 90 different foods in their first year. Remember that spices, herbs, and oil all count as new foods.

Prep Tips for Baby-Lead Weaning

Your home does not need to turn into a restaurant just to feed your little one. Fortunately, you can incorporate simple hacks into your prep and cooking to make BLW easy, even for the busiest working moms.

Tip #1: Eliminate the fancy recipes. Babies are better off with simple single ingredients. It is unlikely that your child will notice if you spend two minutes cutting up a few leftovers vs. making a tofu scramble with quinoa, avocado, and sweet potato. There is no such thing as a foodie baby. Even the simplest food will activate all their senses.

Once your child starts to get the hang of eating, gradually incorporate mixed dishes into their meals. The bottom line is to give plenty of time for the baby to explore each food and develop a liking for food from all food groups.

Tip #2: Dine together as much as possible. If you are eating sweet potato fries, steak, and broccoli, your baby can enjoy these foods too. If you are making hamburgers for the family, make a few in the shape of a finger and eliminate the salt. Any meal can be quickly and easily altered to make it BLW approved. Anytime your baby reaches for something that you are eating, offer a little to them.

Tip #3: Eliminate the salt, sugar, and artificial flavors. Cook and prepare all meals salt-free and then add table salt to adult meals at the end. This ensures that you and your baby can share all meals. Babies' kidneys are not mature enough to deal with added sugar, salt, or artificial flavors in their food.[3]

Tip #4: Add flavor with herbs, spices, and oil. Babies have probably already been exposed to these tastes and flavors while in their mothers' tummies. Many flavors of foods are present in breast milk, too.[4] Babies who drink breast milk are naturally inclined toward different flavors. Those fed formulas may take some time adapting to these flavors, as they are not found in store-bought formula.

Keep in mind that hot and aromatic spices are different. Although you should avoid serving your baby taco, curry, or chili seasoning, there are a lot of spices that they will enjoy. Aromatic spices like cumin, cinnamon, oregano, nutmeg, and dill can be instrumental in developing your child's palette. The idea is not to spice up their food, but to expose them to more flavors.[5] Hold off on hot spices like cayenne and chili powder until three years of age.

Oils such as olive oil, coconut oil, butter, tallow, and ghee can also be used during cooking to add healthy fats and flavor to any meal.

Tip #5: Make it easier on your baby. Some foods will be more slippery than others, and your baby might find it challenging to grasp them. To make foods easier to grasp, purchase a crinkle cutter, giving a wave-like curvy shape to the outside of the food.

For extra slippery foods, like avocados and bananas, you might want to coat them with wholegrain powders to make them less slippery. You can also wash the peel and leave some of it on so they have a non-slippery place to grab.

Cooking Guidelines for Baby-Led Weaning

Here is a general guideline on how you should cook the following foods:

Hard vegetables/fruits: Typically, all hard vegetables and fruits can be steamed, baked, boiled, or sautéed until soft. It is usually easier to cut them into an approved shape prior to cooking.

Bread: Lightly toast or serve un-toasted.

Pasta: Boil until soft, should be overcooked.

Beans/Legumes: Cook until soft and mash into puree or form into patties.

Tofu: Bake, sautée, or serve raw.

Egg: Boil, scramble, or bake. White and yellow should be fully set (well done).

Cheese: Pasteurized cheese can be served raw or included in other meals, like an omelet. All dairy products, including cheese, should contain full fat.

Meat: Slow-cooked or tender stew meat is excellent baby food. Steak can be cut into strips for sucking, and ground meat can be formed into long meatballs. Bigger bones with meat on them that your baby can gnaw on are also okay. Remove gristle, skin, and small, pointy bones after cooking.

Fish: Bake, broil, BBQ, or pan-sear. Try to select low mercury fish such as sardines, mackerel, salmon, trout, herring, cod, and pollock. Fish that easily flakes will be easier for your baby to consume initially. Limit to one to two servings of fish per week.

All meat/fish should be subjected to an internal temperature and should be at least medium-well done.[6]

- Shellfish: 165° F/74° C
- Poultry (whole): 180° F/82° C
- Beef/veal/lamb: 170°F/77°C
- Ground beef/veal/lamb/pork/poultry: 165° F/71° C
- Fish: 158° F/70° C
- Pork: 160-165° F/71° C
- Liver: 165° F/74° C
- Meat/fish leftovers: 165°F/74° C; reheat only once

How to Form a Well Balanced Baby-Led Weaning Meal

When you are ready to start feeding your baby proper meals, rather than single ingredients, you will probably wonder about the best way to make every meal nutritious and well-rounded.

In Dr. Clara Davis's extensive research, she offered infants a variety of healthy foods and allowed them to eat whatever they wanted.

Although each baby ate drastically different diets with weird combinations and larger quantities of particular foods, they all put together a nutritious diet.[7]

Of course, it's not always that simple, but the key takeaway was that when children were provided with only whole foods, they instinctively knew what to eat to become and stay healthy.

The easiest way to put together a meal that supports Davis's research and follows the USDA MyPlate guidelines is to focus on five food groups: protein, starch, fruits/vegetables, fat, and calcium.[8] Although babies get a ton of fat and calcium from breast milk or formula, it is good to get in the habit of including these foods for when your baby turns one and dramatically reduces their milk intake and/or is not willing to drink whole cow's milk.

With each meal, aim to provide three to four foods that include proteins, starch, fruits/vegetables, fat, and calcium. Many foods will fall into two of these categories; for example, full-fat yogurt will be high in fat and calcium. When selecting foods, keep in mind which foods are high in iron and try to incorporate at least one food that is higher in iron with each meal.

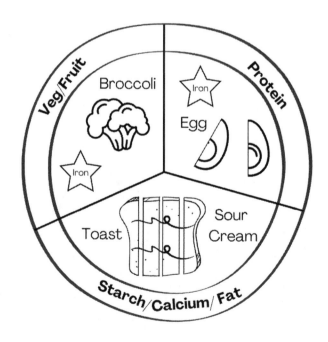

Use this as a guide, but don't worry too much about getting every food group in every meal. Preparing food for your child doesn't need to be a science. Instead, focus on providing as many whole foods as possible. If you would like more guidance, detailed meal ideas can be found in Chapter 9.

Now that we've got that sorted out, you're probably asking yourself, *Is my child really going to eat their vegetables?* Unfortunately, babies are like many adults, and may not go for vegetables. In order to encourage your child's taste for vegetables, offer them first and allow them to get used to their flavor. Fruits can be introduced anytime, and they will likely have a very quick adoption due to their sweetness.

When shopping for baby foods, it is also important to keep in mind that an infant's body is still developing and is much smaller than an adult's. They can be far more sensitive to pesticides and other chemicals in foods. Stick to organic products as much as possible and wash all fruits and vegetables before use.

The Environment Working Group lists the "dirty dozen" every year, and that includes the top twelve pesticide-containing foods. If you can't afford to buy everything organic, try to buy at least these foods organic. Check out the current list here:

https://www.ewg.org/foodnews/dirty-dozen.php

What's the Deal With Iron?

Iron is the one nutrient that you need to pay attention to while weaning your baby. In North America, it is recommended that parents serve their babies 11 mg of iron per day from six to eleven months of age, and then seven mg per day from one year onward.[9] In the UK, the recommendation is 7.8 mg from seven to twelve months of age.[10]

It is unnecessary to count every mg of iron you offer your child, but rather make sure you include high iron foods in as many meals as you can. Introducing meat during the first few weeks is one of the best ways to provide adequate iron, zinc, and vitamin B12. Even if your baby cannot chew and swallow meat, the juices in meat have a high iron content.

Here are the top foods that contain iron that should be incorporated into your baby's diet regularly:[11]

Meat:

- Beef (1 oz = 1 mg)
- Lamb (1 oz = 0.5 mg)
- Bison (1 oz = 1.1 mg)
- Pork (1 oz = 0.3 mg)
- Veal (1 oz = 0.3 mg)
- Chicken Liver (1 oz = 2.6 mg)
- Chicken (1 oz = 0.3 mg)
- Turkey (1 oz = 0.7 mg)

Fish:

- Clams (1 oz = 8 mg)
- Shrimp (1 oz = 0.9 mg)
- Sardines (1 oz = 0.8 mg)
- Salmon (1 oz = 0.3 mg)
- Tuna — canned light (1 oz = 0.5 mg)

Eggs (1 egg = 0.6 mg)

Legumes:

- Chickpeas (¼ cup = 3.1 mg)
- Lentils (¼ cup cooked = 1.7 mg)
- Kidney Beans (¼ cup = 1 mg)
- Black beans (¼ cup = 0.9 mg)

Nuts & Seeds:

- Almonds (1 tbsp = 0.6 mg)
- Cashews (1 tbsp = 0.8 mg)

Vegetables:

- Cooked spinach (½ cup = 1.9 mg)
- Broccoli (½ cup = 0.5 mg)
- Brussels sprouts (½ cup = 0.6 mg)
- Green peas (½ cup = 1 mg)
- Potato (½ cup = 0.6 mg)
- Sweet Potato (½ cup = 0.4 mg)

Tofu (3 oz = 2.2 mg)

Blackstrap Molasses (1 tbsp = 0.9 mg)

Grains and Cereals:

- Iron-fortified cereals (¼ cup = 3.7 – 6 mg depending on the brand)
- Oats (½ cup = 1.7 mg)
- Wholegrain breads (1 slice = 0.7mg)
- Quinoa (½ cup = 1.4 mg)

Fruit:

- Dried apricots – soaked and blended (¼ cup = 1.9 mg)
- Raisins – soaked and blended (1 oz = 0.8 mg)

Hemp hearts (1 tbsp = 1.4mg)

All of the foods above will have a different absorption rate. However, you can quickly improve this rate by combining iron with vitamin C. These two combined together increase the solubility of iron in the small intestines, resulting in a higher absorption rate.[12] Vitamin C is found abundantly in fruits and vegetables like citrus, berries, Brussel sprouts, and bell peppers. On the other hand, combining iron with calcium decreases the absorption rate because they compete for the same receptors in the small intestine.[13]

Iron deficiency can affect your baby's overall health, reduce immune system function, and cause delays in cognitive development.[14] Although iron needs usually are easily met with a BLW or pureed food diet, it is important to be aware of what low iron signs look like.

Signs of iron deficiency:[15]

- Fussiness or irritability
- Fast heartbeat
- Pale skin
- Desire to eat odd substances, like dirt
- Enlarged spleen
- Lack of energy, easily tired
- Sore or swollen tongue

Preventing Allergies

With food allergies affecting nearly 8 percent of children, it is on the forefront of most parents' minds as they start introducing food.[16] A food allergy is defined as anytime the body's immune system reacts unusually to a specific food.[17] Although your child could be allergic to any food, the most common and the ones you should focus on through your weaning journey are the Big 8.[18]

- Peanuts
- Tree Nuts
- Eggs
- Shellfish
- Milk
- Fish
- Wheat
- Soy

There is no surefire way to eliminate your baby's risk of becoming allergic to these foods, but an early introduction is the best prevention. According to a 2010 study, babies introduced to eggs between four and six months were less likely to develop an egg allergy.[19]

Furthermore, a 2016 randomized control "found that the introduction of peanut at 4–11 months of age significantly reduced the risk of developing peanut allergy in high-risk infants."[20]Although past guidelines have recommended waiting to introduce potential allergens, there has been enough supporting evidence that the 2020-2025 Dietary Guidelines now recommend introducing allergens early.[21]

If your family has a high risk of food allergies, seasonal allergies, asthma or eczema, offering these riskier foods in the form of purees can be a great way to get an early introduction at four to six months of age. Even if you don't feel like your child is at high risk of allergies, some of the first solid foods you introduce at six months should be from the Big 8.

When you introduce an allergen, offer it separately from other foods, so you can gauge any reaction. Most symptoms will occur within the first two hours, and it is highly uncommon for an infant to have a severe reaction at the first exposure. Although food rubbed onto the skin can cause irritation, this is irrelevant to any allergic reactions. For an allergy to be tested, your baby must swallow the food.[22]

Liquids such as peanut oil or soy sauce also do not contain enough protein to provide sufficient allergy exposure. Here are potential reactions to look out for:[23]

Mild signs of an allergic reaction:

- Hives
- Skin swelling
- Tongue swelling
- Sneezing
- Throat tightness
- Vomiting
- Stomach pain
- Diarrhea
- Runny nose

Severe signs of an allergic reaction:

- Wheezing

- Difficulty swallowing
- Swelling of the mouth
- Loss of consciousness

It is also important to note that reactions can occur on the second or subsequent exposure, so continue to watch for any unusual symptoms every time you offer these foods.[24] If your child has a severe reaction, call 911 and seek immediate medical assistance. If your child has a mild reaction when exposed to a food, refrain from offering it again until a doctor can perform a skin prick or blood test to determine if they are allergic to the suspected food.

If your child has no symptoms of being allergic, continue to maintain the food as part of their regular diets or roughly one to two times a week.

How to Prepare and Select Purees

Whether you decide to strictly do BLW or incorporate more purees, you will still offer foods like applesauce, mashed beans, and yogurt. By incorporating these foods, you are providing a much-needed variety in textures. When spoon-feeding, it is important to select a consistency that is safe for your baby's skill level. Here are three different puree textures that you can offer to provide variety.[25]

- **Thin puree**: Anything that has been blended or mashed into a smooth consistency. Foods can easily be mixed with breast milk, formula, or water to make a slightly thinner consistency. Typically, a thin puree is only slightly thicker than formula or breast milk, and will drip off a spoon.
- **Thick puree**: Once your child has mastered thin purees, you can gradually increase the thickness by reducing the amount of liquid mixed in or selecting drier foods. Homemade refried beans or hummus are considered thick purees because they are still smooth and uniform in their consistency, but are denser and slightly harder to swallow.
- **Lumpy puree**: Mash foods with a fork or potato masher instead of blending them. This will achieve the consistency of a chunky puree. Start with an easier food, like a banana

mashed with a fork, and move on to foods that have firmer lumps over time, like cottage cheese.

Although we have been focusing on unprocessed whole foods, store-bought purees are still the number one food most babies consume during weaning. In fact, there are a lot of really good purees out there if you know what to look for.

In general, store-bought purees are put into three categories:[26]

Stage 1: Purees that are thin and have a drippy consistency, often having only one ingredient.

Stage 2: Purees that are slightly thicker and have complex flavors with several ingredients.

Stage 3: Mashed food with a lot of texture.

When you introduce purees for the first time, you always want to start with stage 1 and gradually move on to stage 2 and stage 3 over time as your baby's skills develop.

As a general rule of thumb, look for purees that have recognizable ingredients. They should contain whole foods and be devoid of any salt, sugar, or any other artificial ingredients.

Once you open store-bought baby food, most jars can be stored in the fridge for up to three days. If you are new to feeding puree or do not think your baby will eat the entire jar, then refrain from feeding them directly from the jar to avoid any unwanted bacteria. Serve the food into a bowl using a clean spoon.

Along with purees, baby cereal is also an excellent store-bought option for babies when spoon-feeding. Most will contain extra iron and can easily be made into a mushy consistency by adding formula or breast milk, depending on your preference.

If you are replacing a BLW meal with a puree, it is recommended to feed roughly 2-4 oz of a puree per meal.[27] However, your baby will eat as much as they want. It is okay if they are hungry for more or less.

Preparing, cooking, and selecting BLW foods or purees can take some getting used to, but after a week or two, you'll be doing it in your sleep. If you have decided that your baby is ready to start weaning, head to the grocery store or look around your house for foods you already have, and let's get started. It's game time!

Chapter 5
Game Time!

Now that you know about BLW and its basics, you're ready to get your little one munching on some simple snacks. Remember that you want to pick either spoon feeding or BLW at the beginning of each meal, and not both at the same time. Let your child learn and explore one food at a time. Placing a bowl of pasta with cheese and meatballs mixed in may not be the best learning tool early on.

Let's Get Started

For your very first BLW meal, select a vegetable such as cooked carrots, broccoli florets, or avocado spears, and prepare one or two slices or florets. Confirm that they are big enough to prevent your baby from shoving the whole thing in their mouth, but also small enough that they can grasp the slice—roughly the size of an adult finger. Let the food cool to a warm temperature and taste it yourself before serving to make sure it is not too hot.

For more detail on the best first foods to serve, a week one meal plan for BLW can be found in Chapter 9.

Next, support your baby by setting them up for success. A parent in a good mood creates a positive environment that is ideal for learning. Remove any distractions and make sure you have blocked out 30-45 minutes so you can stay with your baby and supervise. You also want to make sure that your baby is happy and has been fed within the last 45-90 minutes. It is hard for your baby to learn a new skill when they are hungry, grumpy, or tired. Feel free to sit down and eat with them; remember, BLW gives your baby a seat at the table.

Now that you have ensured everyone is happy, wash your baby's hands and place them in their highchair. It is essential to make sure they are in a secure and safe position where they feel comfortable. Hips and knees should be at a right angle to prevent your child from leaning back, which can increase their choking risk. Fasten any straps to keep them secure.

Place your slices of prepared vegetables on the highchair tray or a specialized baby-led weaning bowl or plate.

As your baby explores, keep an eye on them in case they need your assistance, but refrain from staring, laughing, or pointing. You want your child to be able to do their own thing without feeling any pressure from you.

Lastly, remember to only clean once your child has finished eating. Leave all the food on the baby's mouth, hands, and tray until they are entirely finished, unless you're removing pieces of food that have become too small and could be a potential choking hazard. It's important for babies to feel their food and get messy.

What to Expect

Through this process, your child will learn several new skills and venture into new territory. Therefore, it is essential to know what to expect and how they will react to new tastes, smells, and textures.

To pique your child's interest and ensure that they look forward to eating instead of dreading it, let them have fun. It's not always enjoyable watching food get smashed, smeared, and thrown around your house, but know that it's the best way for your child to learn this powerful new skill of eating. The more colors and textures you provide your infant with (at a reasonable pace), the more fun they will have exploring.

BLW behaviors you should expect from your child:

- Licking
- Tasting
- Exploring
- Refusing some foods
- Spitting out some foods
- Coughing
- Gagging as they learn how to chew and swallow (safe and natural for an infant)
- Not a lot of eating or swallowing for the first month or two

Parents' Mindset

We live so much of our adult lives in a hurry, and that mindset can be very overwhelming for an infant. Give your child whatever time they need to complete a BLW meal. Baby-led weaning cannot be rushed!

It is also okay when your baby rejects a food. Over time, the more you expose them to various foods, the more they will acquire a taste for something they previously disliked. Don't ever give up on a particular food. You can hold off on a food for a while and try again in a few days or weeks. Never rush your baby if they aren't comfortable. Acquiring a taste for a food is a process that takes place at your baby's pace. Take it slow and enjoy the journey.

Eating should also be a very normal activity in your household. It should never be used as a bribe, punishment, or reward. Using sayings like "Just one more bite" encourages the baby to eat more than they can stomach. Anything that praises, pressures, or scolds a child around eating should be removed entirely from your vocabulary. These words are what encourage kids to overeat, undereat, and become picky eaters. Remember, eating is essential, and nothing about it is good or bad. Your baby intuitively knows how to get enough food to support all their needs if you let them control their eating.

In order to foster a healthy environment around food, you must remain neutral about different foods and let your little one explore on their own. Parents who have struggled with bottle aversion or picky eating can use BLW to foster positive emotions around food. It is also likely that your baby will mimic your actions and reactions. While it is very beneficial to show them how to eat, they will also imitate your responses to food. Remain neutral if you try a food you don't like and try not to show too much excitement over your favorite flavor of ice cream.

Lastly, be aware that some food will be wasted. You can minimize this by only giving a few pieces of each food at a time and picking up any food that has been dropped on a clean surface and giving it back to them. After a few weeks, your baby's coordination will improve, and less food will be wasted every day. If you use purees and do a combo method, anything not eaten or smashed can also be blended and stored for the next meal.

Possible Outcomes

Many different situations could arise during BLW meals, and I want to prepare you for all of them. The more you know, the more confident you will be. Here are the possible outcomes of your baby exploring solid food, accompanied by tips on how to respond:

1. Baby bites off more than they can chew (literally) and gags/coughs.

Gagging will help your child learn which foods they can safely eat and how much they can put in their mouth. This is completely normal and an essential part of the learning process. Solid food will help move the gag reflex back, which will allow the baby to hold more food in their mouth over time as they get more practice.

Remember the below saying so you know when to be concerned:

"Loud and red, let them go ahead. Silent and blue, they need help from you."

If you feel uneasy about gagging, one way to prevent frequent gagging in the beginning is to provide harder foods that they can nibble but can't completely bite off. Try giving them a rib, mango pit, bell pepper, or cucumber.

2. Baby eats a portion of the food, so there is only a tiny piece left.

Small pieces significantly increase your child's risk of choking. In the beginning, once your child has eaten a decent amount of the piece of food you have provided, remove it and replace it with a bigger piece. Broccoli is a great example; once your baby has eaten the floret, remove the stem. These smaller pieces can be blended or pureed so they don't go to waste.

3. Baby seems unsatisfied after a meal.

If your child seems like they're still hungry after they have finished their meal, you might want to consider offering purees for their next meal; that's the beauty of this combination method. If a child doesn't have enough skills to chew and swallow some foods successfully, they might be left unsatisfied. If this happens it might be beneficial to incorporate some purees, but never immediately after solid foods. Otherwise, your baby may learn that they will still get purees if they don't eat their solid food.

4. Baby is unsuccessful at picking the food up or bringing it to their mouth.

Although it is not necessary, feel free to help your child hold the food in the beginning or perform the task for them so they can imitate you. For example, a banana is a good fruit that you can assist them with, especially if you find that they are getting flustered. That being said, never put any solid food in your baby's mouth. If your baby cannot bite or gnaw a piece of food on their own, it is likely too challenging for them.

It is also okay if they are happy just playing with the food initially and not ingesting anything. As mentioned earlier, they are getting lots of benefits just by touching and playing with foods. Do not expect any eating for the first few weeks.

5. Baby has no interest in the food or loses interest very quickly.

Some babies take longer to show an interest in food. It might be that your baby doesn't realize that food relieves hunger like formula or breast milk. Take a break from solid food for a few days and keep offering it until they show an interest. Babies who take longer to immerse themselves in food normally progress very quickly once they get going.

6. Baby uses their hands to keep food in their mouth.

Throughout the first few weeks, your baby will be fine-tuning their control of their lips and tongue. Until they are able to curl their lips, they might use their hands to help keep food in their mouth while they swallow. Over time, as their oral-motor skills develop, this behavior should stop.[1]

7. Baby seems frustrated.

There are many reasons why your baby might find eating frustrating. It is a very challenging skill, and they are going to fail a lot more than they succeed in the beginning. Make sure that they have been recently nursed or bottle-fed so they are not hungry.

You might also be giving them food that is too slippery or small to hold. If your child is still frustrated even with large pieces and a full tummy, they might just need more time to practice, and in time, they will figure it out.

8. Baby uses two hands to feed themselves.

As your child works on their coordination, it can be difficult to guide their hand to their mouth successfully. Using one hand to guide the other hand can make it easier to place food in their mouth and improve their accuracy.[2]

9. Baby makes a sharp, loud cry while eating.

It is likely that your baby has just bitten their tongue or finger by accident. While they are learning to make a mental map of their mouth, they might accidentally bite their tongue while moving food around. A finger could also get in the way as they figure out how to successfully bite a piece of food and get it in their mouth.[3]

10. Baby throws or smashes all their food.

This is normally a phase that lasts for only a few days, but you can pick up any food that hasn't been destroyed as long as it falls on a clean surface. Anything that is still intact can be given back to your baby. If most of the foods become smashed or deformed, it can be good to have more food prepared to offer them.

Is Your Baby Succeeding?

The process of eating is quite a lot more complex than we realize. Take a bite, move the food to the side, move your jaw up and down repeatedly to chew and break down your food, and finally move food to the back of your tongue to swallow.

It will take your child a long time to learn this sequence, but they will have small successes along the way that will show them they are getting the hang of it.

Initially, success during weaning is reflected in the progression of your baby's ability to grab a piece of solid food or a pre-filled spoon and bring it to their mouth—but not necessarily put it in their mouth. Over time, they will be able to take bites and get better at chewing and swallowing successfully. Success can be seen in small achievements.

When to Start or Continue a Meal

Although in the beginning, you want to offer food when your child is relatively full so they have the patience to practice, over time, you can offer solid foods when they show signs of hunger. These signs will be different for every baby, so notice anything indicating that they are trying to get your attention. You will also want to learn to recognize the signs that indicate that they want more food during a meal.

Some of the most common signs that your child wants food are:[4]

- Putting their hands to their mouth.
- Smacking their lips.
- Reaching for or pointing to food.
- Getting excited when they see food.
- Using hand motions or sounds to indicate they are still hungry.

- Guiding the spoon with their hands.
- Opening their mouth when offered a spoon.

When to End a Meal

Typically, when a child has finished eating or playing with the food you have offered, it is pretty obvious because they won't show any interest in it anymore. It is important to stop feeding at the first sign of fullness. Encouraging your child to eat more when they are satiated or have lost interest in the activity can create negative emotions around eating.

Here are some of the common signs that indicate you can end the meal:[5]

- Getting distracted, not looking at you or the food
- Not opening the mouth
- Turning away from the spoon or food
- Pushing the spoon or food away, like they are giving it back to you
- Spitting out food
- Turning or shaking their head
- Closing their mouth when food is offered
- Starting to fuss
- No longer playing with the solid food

When you end a BLW meal, it is important to check for food pockets in their cheeks, roof of the mouth, and any other crevice. Food can easily get lodged in these areas when a baby overstuffs their mouth. Over time, as they create a mental map of their mouth, they will learn how much food they can actually eat at one time, but in the meantime, you need to check after every meal by asking them to open up wide. If you see excess food, you can offer them a glass of water to help remove the food so they can chew and swallow.

How to Modify Baby-Led Weaning as Your Baby Improves Their Skill

As your child masters one skill, you should continue to challenge them. Every food, texture, and shape will bring a new element that they need to learn. Remember, the goal is for their meals to eventually look similar to an adult's meals.

6-8 months

During the first week or so of BLW, start giving your child multiple different foods in one meal. This will teach them to make choices for themselves and decide which foods they want to eat and which ones they don't want to eat.

Provide some easier foods, and some more challenging foods that require more navigation than simply picking them up from the table and putting them in their mouths. A juicy mango pit is a great example.

Your baby should be able to pick up foods with their whole palm and eat anything that is poking out of their hand. Their accuracy and ability to bring foods to their mouth should also improve dramatically during this time. You might notice that they don't crush a food when they pick it up and can gauge how hard they need to squeeze to successfully pick up softer foods.[6]

8-9 months

Around eight to nine months, your child will develop more hand and mouth control. As they gnaw different foods, they should be able to keep things in their mouth longer and successfully swallow more foods. You might also notice visible teeth. With their new pearly whites, your child may now be able to tear foods. Teeth will allow more versatility and should help your child to break down crunchier or slightly harder foods.

At this age, children also start to develop what is commonly called a pincer grasp. This is when they can grasp items with a lot more precision using their thumb and index finger.[7] Each time you hold a pen or button a shirt, your pincer grasp is in play.

Pincer Grasp

It may seem like a very natural movement for an adult but it is an essential milestone in developing a child's fine motor skills. At this point, chop up foods into smaller half-inch by half-inch cubes (1.3 x 1.3 cm) so that they can get plenty of practice.

To scale food size and shape for 9+ month old babies (pincer grasp)

Although they will be much better at chewing and swallowing at this stage and less likely to choke, avoid serving anything in a round or coin shape.

You can also start to get more creative by offering purees and sauces for dipping.

12 months

By the time your child turns one, transition away from spoon-feeding if you have been incorporating it up until this point. Continue to leave out salt and sugar, but they should be able to eat almost everything else at this age.[8] Feel free to experiment with firmer foods and different shapes. However, hard foods will still need to be cooked.

This is also a great time to introduce a fork and other utensils. If they are already familiar with a spoon, they should be able to learn how to use a fork very quickly. Your child might prefer one over the other for picking things up.

When you introduce cutlery, make sure you don't leave them unsupervised as they may hurt themselves. Learning how to use cutlery can be as slow as learning how to eat. Most babies will resort to their hands in the beginning because they are much easier to eat with.

Expected Changes

Expect several changes in your child as they move from an all-milk diet to purees and other solid foods. They are figuring out how to chew and ingest, and their young digestive systems are slowly adapting.

The most noticeable change will be in their bowel movements. Remember that each baby is different, and there is no "correct" number of times your baby will pass stool. The goal here is not how many times but that they have a smooth and stress-free poop.

Stools will become more solid and fluctuate in color, much like adults' stools. Be prepared to face stronger smelling poop. The appearance will change based on the digestibility of what they eat. It is normal to spot undigested pieces of food, like skins of vegetables, the hull of corn, or even a whole, unchanged kernel. It is also likely that your child will start to poop less than before.[9]

There is a chance of constipation during the weaning process. A decrease in bowel movements can be remedied by ensuring that your baby is hydrated, providing a quick belly massage, or serving an extra helping of fruits, such as pears and apples. Fruit juices like prune juice can also be used, but dilute them with water by at least a half.

If your child's stool is more on the liquid side than the solid, their digestive tract may need some time to heal. Reduce the amount of solid food and try spacing out solids over a few days.

What About Water?

Although it is not necessary, you can offer water after six months of age. The American Academy of Pediatrics suggests offering up to eight oz per day, but most children will not consume more than two to four oz while weaning.[10] Surprisingly, water is one of the hardest liquids to learn how to drink because it is so much thinner than breast milk and formula.

Learning how to drink water is an excellent way for your child to get an oral workout. It is important only to offer water during meals, so it doesn't interfere with formula or breast milk consumption. Starting at the age of six months, offering water using two different methods is recommended to further help motor and drinking skills.

Method 1: Drinking out of a cup

Sippy cups are normally what parents think they are supposed to introduce first, but did you know that they were invented by a dad that just wanted to keep his carpets clean! Although they do a great job of preventing spills, they prevent the tongue from lifting toward the roof of the mouth, which makes it hard to swallow. Over time, this can cause a delay in oral-motor development.[11]

Instead, opt for a small cup that your child can easily grasp and that only holds a few ounces of water. Fill it up so they won't have to tip it too far to drink. Offer it to your child and wait until they actively engage by placing their hands on the cup. Next, assist them with bringing it to their mouth. It will take a lot of practice and trial and error, so be prepared for some spills initially. Their skills will develop quickly once they get the hang of it.[12]

Method 2: Drinking out of a straw

Drinking out of a straw is another common way that adults drink beverages, so it will be important to introduce a straw from an early age as well. You might notice that your baby is able to pick up this skill a lot faster than drinking from a cup because they have a strong sucking reflex.

In order to encourage your child to drink from a straw, fill a standard plastic straw with a little bit of liquid and hold your finger on the bottom to prevent it from falling out. Once your baby sees the straw and opens their mouth, gently place it in their mouth and release the small amount of liquid into their mouth.

Once your baby realizes that liquid comes out of the straw, transition to a cup and straw and continue to assist as they learn. In order to successfully remove the liquids, their lips need to close, their tongue must retract, and their cheeks must tighten. Offer thicker liquids, such as a smoothie, once your child is comfortable with water.[13]

If your child shows no interest in cup or straw drinking and is under the age of eight months, just keep offering it during every meal, and wait until they show interest.

It is normal to feel a little nervous about your first baby-led weaning meal, but I think you will be surprised by how well it goes. Over the next few months, you will see some rapid growth and development from your baby, and it should be fascinating to watch. Every meal they successfully eat will feel like a huge accomplishment for both of you.

Chapter 6
What to Offer Based on Age and Skill Level

There is never a one-size-fits-all when it comes to introducing solid food. Every baby is different. That being said, it can be helpful to have some basic guidelines to get you started. Below, I have outlined foods that are safe based on age and your child's abilities. They are designed to give you ideas of healthy options. Use these as inspiration and a chance to expose your child to foods you might not have initially thought to serve.

Beginner Purees: 4-6 months of age

The first purees that you offer your child should be very thin and normally made with a single ingredient. Your child should be able to easily swallow the puree because it is only slightly more challenging than formula or breast milk. If you are making a puree from home, you want it to be thin enough that it drips off the spoon. An easy and effective way to do this is to blend the food of choice with breast milk, formula, or water.

- Carrot puree
- Banana puree
- Avocado puree
- Pumpkin puree

- Pear puree
- Peach puree
- Sweet potato puree
- Green bean puree
- Pea puree
- Squash puree
- Meat puree
- Baby oatmeal—store-bought
- Rice cereal—store-bought
- Stage 1 purees—store-bought

Beginner BLW—6 months old or first introduction to solid food

All of the foods below are great to start with if you are new to BLW. Start with foods that are mild in taste and easy for your baby to digest. Your baby's digestive system will be developed enough to handle most foods by six months, so do not be limited to the foods listed below. An intermediate food might be okay for your beginner baby; these lists are only designed to give you a rough outline.

Feel free to add approved spices and healthy fats when cooking as your baby gets familiar with foods, so you can include additional tastes and textures. It can be easy to second-guess yourself with each meal, wondering if you have cooked and cut the food properly, but as long as you follow these two rules, you will be in the clear.

#1 Foods need to be soft enough so they can easily be squished between your fingers.

#2 Foods should be cut into strips the size of an adult finger, like a spear.

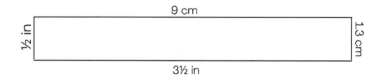

Vegetables/fruits that need to be cooked:

- Sweet potato fries
- Zucchini spears—seeds removed
- Butternut squash spears
- Carrot spears—avoid baby carrots
- Broccoli florets—remove the stem from baby's plate once floret is eaten
- Cauliflower florets—remove the stem from baby's plate once floret is eaten
- Beet spears
- Pumpkin spears
- Parsnip spears
- Apple spears—skin removed

Raw squishy foods: Must be ripe and soft. You can wash the skin or peel it and leave some on or dust the food with dried grains to make it easier for your child to hold.

- Banana—Cut in half and remove some of the peel so baby can suck on it like a Popsicle; just expose enough food for your baby to gnaw on.
- Avocado spears
- Mango spears
- Melon spears
- Pear spears
- Peach/nectarine spears
- Watermelon spears—seeds removed

Raw firm foods: Designed only for sucking on

- Cucumber spears—seeds removed
- Red pepper spears—yellow, red, orange, or green
- Jicama spears—remove skin

Dairy, eggs, meat, and fish:

- Hard-boiled egg—quartered

- Omelet—just egg, cut into strips
- Ground beef, lamb, pork, chicken, or turkey—shaped into long, thin meatball
- Steaks or chops—choose a tender cut of meat and cut against the grain into strips. Ensure that the piece will stay together and will not fall apart. These are purely for sucking on.
- Ribs
- Chicken or turkey breasts/thighs—tear or cut into strips
- Fish—remove bones and cut into strips against the grain
- Mozzarella spears
- Sour cream—use as a spread or make a dip
- Cream cheese—use as a spread or make a dip
- Mascarpone cheese—use as a spread or make a dip
- Goat Cheese—use as a spread or make a dip
- Cheddar cheese strip
- Jack cheese strip
- Swiss cheese strip
- Yogurt

Other:

- Tofu strips—raw or cooked
- Toast—lightly toasted and cut into strips
- English muffin—lightly toasted and cut into strips
- Pita bread—lightly toasted and cut into strips
- Sticky rice—formed into the shape of an adult finger
- Pancakes—homemade and cut into strips(see recipe in Chapter 8)
- Nut butter—mix smooth nut butter with water to make a yogurt consistency
- Unsweetened applesauce

Spices: fresh or dried

- Basil
- Cilantro
- Parsley

- Cloves
- Saffron
- Cardamom
- Nutmeg
- Cinnamon
- Dill
- Rosemary—slightly pulsed or ground
- Cumin
- Oregano
- Thyme
- Mint
- Turmeric
- Ginger

Oils—for cooking or sauces

- Olive oil
- Coconut oil
- Butter
- Tallow
- Ghee
- Avocado oil

Intermediate Purees: 6-8 Months

Once your child has mastered thinner purees, you can increase the thickness of the puree to make it slightly more challenging. By adding less liquid or no liquid, most foods have a thick, creamy consistency when pureed or blended. Start by purchasing or pureeing food that they are already familiar with, just with a thicker texture. From there, add additional foods like the ones below and also incorporate multiple ingredient purees for variety.

- Carrot puree
- Chickpea puree
- Broccoli puree
- Zucchini puree
- Blueberry puree

- Mango puree
- Durian puree
- Dried apricot puree—soaked and blended
- Raisin puree—soaked and blended
- Beet puree
- Parsnip puree
- Persimmon puree
- Edamame puree
- Asparagus puree
- Black bean puree
- Lentil puree
- Hummus
- Fish puree
- Ricotta cheese
- Quark cheese
- Mashed egg yolks—mix with water to make a yogurt consistency
- Quinoa puree
- Nut butter—mix smooth nut butter with water to make a yogurt consistency
- Unsweetened applesauce
- Whole milk plain yogurt
- Stage 2 store-bought purees: multiple ingredients

Intermediate BLW: 7-8 months

Once your child has been exposed to beginner BLW foods for a few weeks, you can start introducing more foods to provide additional variety. At this stage, you can start to introduce foods that are slightly more acidic as well.

You should see significant improvement in your child's skills over the next month. They will still be learning how to move food side-to-side and forward and backward in their mouth, but they should be swallowing more food every day. They will also be fine-tuning their grip strength by learning how hard they need to squeeze an object to pick it up without squishing it.

Vegetables/fruits that need to be cooked:

- Green beans—whole and large
- Brussels sprouts—larger than a baby's mouth or cut in wedges
- Eggplant—skin removed
- Bok choy leaves
- Plantain spears
- Spaghetti squash
- White potato fries
- Turnip spears
- Portabella mushroom strips
- Button mushrooms—larger than a baby's mouth or cut in wedges
- Okra—large
- Rutabaga spears
- Daikon radish spears
- Sunchoke spears
- Cassava root spears

Raw squishy foods: must be ripe and soft

- Figs—halved
- Mango spears
- Kiwi wedges
- Plum spears
- Apricot wedges
- Pineapple strips
- Strawberry—larger than a baby's mouth
- Persimmon wedges
- Tomato wedges—skin removed
- Green onion/scallion—whole

Dairy, eggs, meat, and fish:

- Mackerel (boneless & skinless)
- Sardines (boneless & skinless)
- Tongue strips

- Liver strips
- Duck strips
- Venison strips
- Lamb strips
- Bone marrow—used as a spread .

Other:

- Toast strips with a spread
- Overcooked wholewheat or lentil pasta—penne, bowtie, fusilli, large shells
- Tempeh strips
- Nutritional yeast—used in recipes
- Coconut flakes—used in recipes
- Sesame seeds, chia seeds, or hemp hearts—used in recipes or mixed in yogurt
- Ground flax—used in recipes
- Blended nuts—use in muffins, pancakes, oatmeal, or smoothies
- Lentils—in a bowl to scoop up with hands

Advanced Purees: 8-10 months

At this stage, you can transition from pureeing and blending most foods to mashing. Your child is likely ready for more of a challenge. Foods can have a lot more texture and be slightly chunky. Continue to feed all the same foods from the beginner and intermediate stages; just prepare them differently. Most foods can be mashed with a fork or slightly pulsed in a food processor. An advanced puree should have some smooth parts with chunks of bigger soft foods. Purees that are slightly more acidic can also be introduced at this time.

- Mashed kiwi
- Mashed strawberry
- Pineapple puree
- Cooked spinach puree
- Mashed steamed peas

- Cottage cheese
- Tomato sauce (no added sugar)
- Mashed cooked rhubarb
- Mashed pasta or rice
- Shredded meat
- Lobster or crab puree
- Scrambled eggs
- Mashed polenta
- Smoothies
- Stage 3 store-bought puree

Advanced BLW: 9-12 months

By nine months of age, your baby should start practicing their pincer grasp by using their thumb and index finger to pick items up. Although you still want to avoid round foods that could cause choking, you can begin offering food cut into half-inch cubes (1.3 x 1.3 cm).

You might notice that your child can lick their lips, take bigger bites, and successfully swallow more foods. Continue to offer all the same foods from the baby-led weaning beginner and intermediate stages, but cut the foods in cubes instead of strips. This is also a great time to offer dips and sauces for vegetable sticks. Take these last few months before your baby turns one to continue to focus on variety and introducing them to as many foods as possible.

Vegetables/fruits that need to be cooked:

- Edamame—cut in half
- Asparagus spears
- Leeks—chopped finely and used in recipes
- Collard greens—chopped finely and used in recipes

- Cabbage strips
- Tomatillos—used in recipes
- Artichoke heart wedges
- Swiss chard—chopped finely and used in recipes
- Peas—steamed and flattened between fingers
- Spinach—chopped finely and used in recipes
- Snap peas
- Onions—chopped finely and used in recipes
- Corn on the cob—cut into two-inch rounds (5 cm)
- Dried fruit—cut in half, cooked in boiling water until soft

Raw squishy foods:

- Blueberries—flatten between fingers or cut in half
- Blackberries—quarter lengthwise
- Raspberries—flatten between fingers or cut in half
- Grapes—quarter lengthwise
- Papaya spears
- Orange wedges—seeds removed, serve with or without peel
- Grapefruit—seeds removed, serve with or without peel
- Cherries—pitted and cut in quarters
- Strawberries—thinly sliced
- Tomato—thinly sliced
- Olives (in water)—quarter lengthwise
- Lychees (in water)—quarter lengthwise
- Pickle spears (no salt)
- Capers—flatten between fingers

Dairy, eggs, meat, and fish:

- Shredded chicken, beef, or pork
- Octopus—cut into half-inch pieces (1.3 cm)
- Squid—cut into half-inch pieces (1.3 cm)
- Escargot—cut in half
- Meatballs—halved
- Shrimp—tail and shell removed, sliced in half lengthwise or chop finely for recipes
- Crab

- Sausage—low sugar/sodium and quarter lengthwise
- Kidneys
- Caviar/Roe
- Anchovies (in water)—whole
- Feta—crumbled

Other:

- Couscous
- Basmati rice
- Chickpeas—flatten between fingers
- Quinoa
- Seaweed sheets—ripped into strips
- Oysters—cut into half-inch pieces (1.3 cm)
- Lemon/lime—use with recipes
- Bone broth—in a cup

Meals: Transition into combined foods instead of single food items

- Hummus with carrots
- Grilled cheese cut into small squares
- Mashed beans, grated cheese, chopped tomato and tortilla strips
- Pasta with cut-up meatballs, red sauce, and Parmesan cheese
- Quiche—shredded cheese and finely diced vegetables
- Yogurt with a drizzle of diluted almond butter and halved blueberries
- Sautéed spinach with cubed mushrooms
- Casserole—finely diced vegetables and meat
- Quesadilla—with cheese
- Meatloaf
- Oatmeal with cinnamon and shredded apple

12 Months and Beyond

By the time your baby has reached this milestone, they should be able to eat whatever you are eating, assuming your diet is wholesome and well-balanced. Continue to leave out the salt and sugar. Although they will likely still be consuming breast milk or formula, your baby can now have cow's milk as an additional beverage.

Food for Improving Oral-Motor Skills

Every food you introduce will have its own learning curve and challenges, but some food is better at teaching your little one how to eat than others. For your baby to control the food in their mouth and move it around to chew and swallow effectively, they need first to develop a mental map of their mouth.

With a complete mental map, your baby can tell where a food is in their mouth and if it has been chewed enough to swallow. For parents concerned about gagging, offering large, resistant food that can touch every part of their mouth will quickly build this map.[1] These are also safe foods to offer from day one of their BLW journey.

Many foods fit these criteria, but some of my favorites are:[2]

- Mango pits
- Spareribs
- Chicken drumsticks
- Popsicles
- Corn on the cob

All of the above foods can help a baby explore the inside their mouth without fear of choking. These foods will also help with tongue movement, muscle feedback, and touch input. Although it is unlikely that your child will be able to eat any food off these objects in the beginning, view it as an exercise to improve oral skills.

Get Out of Your Comfort Zone:

All parents have their top, go-to foods that they know how to cook and love to eat. Unfortunately, it can be very easy to fall into these same habits when it comes to your child's food. It can be daunting learning how to cook foods you have never heard of before. The good news is that your baby thinks everything you do is amazing, so there is no better time to experiment than now. Offering unique and different foods is a sure way to raise a toddler and adult that eats anything.

Try to experiment with at least one new food a week from the extensive list of foods above. I also highly recommend introducing liver as soon as possible. It is a complex flavor to acquire a taste for later in life, and it is one of the most nutrient-dense foods on the planet. Liver has high levels of vitamin A and can be toxic if consumed in excess. It is recommended to only serve one or two tbsp of liver per week.[3]

Foods You Should Avoid Under 12 Months of Age

- Anything that is in the size and shape of a coin
- Anything hard or crunchy
- Anything with added salt or sugar
- Anything with artificial flavoring, sweeteners, or preservatives
- Prepackaged meals
- Fried food
- Hot and sticky foods
- Raw leafy greens (kale, collards, spinach, bok choy, Swiss chard, lettuce)
- Raw apples
- Raw carrots
- Whole grapes
- Whole cherries
- Cherry tomatoes
- Celery (too stringy)
- Uncooked dried fruit
- Whole nuts and seeds
- Big globs of nut butter
- Scallops (a common source of food poisoning)
- Hot dogs
- Large chunks of meat

- Processed meats (ham, bacon, pepperoni, salami)
- Undercooked meat or fish
- Fish with high levels of mercury (shark, swordfish, marlin)
- Unpasteurized lunchmeat
- Smoked meat and fish
- Fish with bones
- Undercooked egg
- Unpasteurized dairy products
- Large chunks of cheese
- Unpasteurized cheese (brie/blue cheese)
- Cow's milk as a main drink—a small amount can be incorporated into recipes
- Low-fat products—babies need more fat than adults
- Canned soups
- White bread
- Rice milk—contains high levels of arsenic
- Crumbly foods (crackers/chips)
- Unprocessed wheat bran
- Granola
- Popcorn
- Marshmallows
- Pretzels
- Sugar (maple syrup, agave, palm sugar, etc.)
- Honey
- Hard, gooey, or sticky candy
- Fruit juice—unless used for medical purposes like constipation
- Carbonated drinks
- Caffeine (tea, coffee, soda)[4]

Avoiding all these foods will keep your baby safe and dramatically reduce the risk of choking throughout the weaning process.

Chapter 7
Baby-Led Weaning for the Busy Parent

Although it might be hard to believe right now, one of the reasons why parents opt to do BLW is because it is actually easier. When your baby becomes part of your mealtime, it saves you time, money, and energy. It might take you a few days or weeks to get the hang of it, but soon, you'll be able to quickly modify any meal to make it work for your little one.

Follow the guidelines below to make any adult meal baby-led weaning approved:

1. Eliminate the salt and sugar.
2. Eliminate nuts, dried fruit, or other choking hazards from the meal.
3. Cook vegetables a little longer.
4. Cook meats so they are tender.
5. Cut foods in long strips instead of coins.
6. Chop foods until they are extremely fine in mixed dishes.
7. Remove tough skins from poultry or fruits/vegetables (unless the skin is being used to help your baby hold on to the food).
8. Choose longer noodles for pasta, like penne.
9. Shape meatballs, burgers, patties, and fritters into long strips.

10. Pulse any adult meal that is too challenging, e.g. fried rice, casserole, pasta dish. Mix it with an egg or two and bake in patties the shape of an adult finger.

Batch Cooking

In order to always have nutrient-dense meals for the whole family, batch cooking can be a great option. Whenever you are busy and don't have time to cook for the family, this will ensure you always have something in the fridge for all of you to eat. Any of the recipes in Chapter 8, along with anything you cook or cut for BLW, can be doubled and stored in the refrigerator for later. Most foods can be stored in an airtight glass container for two to three days in the fridge. I like to cook extra so there is always something on hand.

Freezing foods is another great option for items that your baby can't eat right away. The easiest way to freeze foods for BLW is to use a method called flash freezing. Simply spread out berries, vegetables, fruits, shredded meat, or anything you can think of on a large baking sheet and place in the freezer for roughly two hours. Then throw all the contents in a freezer-safe Ziploc bag and label with a date. Most items can last up to a month or more in the freezer.

It is always best to defrost any foods in the fridge instead of at room temperature on the counter. You can also pop frozen or defrosted items in the oven, microwave, or toaster until hot, and then let cool until warm. Reheat all food to 165°F/74°C and only reheat once.

Here are some examples of everyday items that you can cook in large quantities and store in the fridge or freezer:

- BBQ chicken breasts
- Muffins
- Hard-boiled eggs
- Meatballs
- Sweet potato fries
- Pancakes
- Berries
- Cooked vegetable sticks

Store-bought Baby-Led Weaning Foods:

Some parents might feel like there is absolutely no way they have time to make one meal a day, much less multiple meals. Luckily, no matter how busy you are, there are ways you can make BLW work for you. All the foods below can be found at almost any grocery store and require either no prep or very minimal prep. Stock up on some of these foods and keep them on hand for when you're short on time.

- Frozen bags of veggies—peas, broccoli, or medley
- Frozen cherries/blueberries
- Frozen butternut squash—if cut in cubes, mash it once cooked
- Frozen sweet potato fries—no salt
- Frozen french fries—no salt
- Frozen shredded hash browns—just potato
- Raw pre-cut vegetable sticks
- Green onions/scallions
- Banana
- Avocado
- Berries
- Edamame
- Packaged roasted beets—not canned
- Jarred mango
- Olives—in water
- Canned pumpkin
- Canned green beans
- Canned artichoke hearts—in water
- Canned pineapple—in water
- Canned mandarin oranges—in water
- Apple sauce—just apple
- Seaweed snacks
- Dried snap peas
- Packaged hard-boiled eggs
- Mozzarella cheese sticks
- Babybel cheese
- Yogurt—plain, full fat

- Yogurt Pouches
- Cottage cheese
- Ricotta
- Cheddar cheese
- Swiss cheese
- Cream cheese
- Goat cheese
- Feta cheese
- Ravioli (low/no salt)
- Pasta (penne, bowtie, fusilli, large shells)
- Pasta sauce —no salt/sugar
- Pita pockets
- Thin rice cakes
- Wholegrain sliced bread (low sodium or no added salt)
- Naan
- Weetabix
- Polenta
- Nut butter (peanut, almond, tahini, cashew)—always dilute
- Rotisserie chicken—no salt/naked
- Chicken strips precooked
- Tuna—no salt
- Sardines—boneless, skinless, and no salt
- Anchovies—in water

Note: Even if you are not doing store-bought purees, check out the baby food aisle. There are tons of finger food snacks that are great options as well.

On the Go! Takeout and Restaurant Options

Purees can be a great option when you are on the go, but you might be surprised by how easy BLW can be as well. There are a lot of items at most restaurants that can be used as finger food, especially under the "sides" section of the menu. Just make sure to ask the waiter to leave out the salt.

In the beginning, it can be helpful to pick items that your baby has tried before. Restaurants have a lot of noise and distractions, so trying to eat something new might be overwhelming. It is also unlikely that you will be able to create a well-balanced meal at a restaurant, so view it purely as playtime and a chance to work on their skills.

- Plain steamed vegetables
- Egg cooked over hard (or scrambled or omelet)
- Pancakes
- Toast, English muffin, or pita bread
- Plain oatmeal
- Hummus
- Guacamole
- Tomato slices
- Corn on the cob
- Beans (smashed between your fingers or with your fork)
- Shredded chicken or pork
- Grilled fish
- Soft tortillas
- Mashed vegetables—potatoes, squash, creamed corn, creamed spinach
- Sweet potato fries
- Breaded appetizers—fish cakes, cheese sticks, veggie croquettes
- Salad with lots of toppings—pick out the toppings that are appropriate for your baby's skill level
- Pasta with tomato or cream sauce

How to Serve Enough Iron

Although it is relatively easy to ensure your baby gets enough iron, it can sometimes be challenging to think of ways to include iron-rich foods in your child's meals. Below are a few ideas on how you can sneak them in there without them even knowing.

- Blend tofu into smoothies.
- Add molasses to baked goods.
- Blend baby cereal or baby oats in a food processor to make them finer and more like flour. Bake with this instead of flour.

- Make meat or liver puree to spread on toast.
- Save any juices that come off meat while it is resting and mix in other dishes instead of water.
- Use cast iron pans.

All of these methods can help you ensure that you get at least one source of a high iron food with every meal. As we already discussed, you can increase the absorption of the iron by serving it with other foods that are high in Vitamin C.

Iron and vitamin C meal ideas:

- Iron-fortified oatmeal with raspberries
- Legumes with sweet potato
- Meat puree with green beans
- Tofu and tomatoes
- Ribs and broccoli florets
- Liver pate with cooked carrots
- Molasses cookies
- Hummus on toast
- Meatballs with squash
- Cereal (fortified with iron) and oranges
- Ground meat with pasta and tomato sauce
- Tofu veggie stir fry with halved peas

How to Introduce the Eight Allergens?

It is important to introduce peanuts, tree nuts, eggs, shellfish, milk, fish, wheat, and soy as early as possible once you start introducing solid foods. In the beginning, it is best to introduce them one by one, so you can look for any allergic signs or symptoms. Once you have concluded that your child is not allergic, make sure to offer these foods consistently. Here are some easy ways to add these foods to everyday meals:

- Use soy milk instead of water when diluting peanut butter, making pancakes, mashing purees, or for any other liquid required in a recipe.
- Purchase soy yogurt.

- Dilute peanut butter, almond butter, cashew butter, etc., and add small quantities to toast, English muffins, pita bread, or purees.
- Grind other tree nuts into a powder and use instead of flour in recipes.
- Peanut Puffs can be purchased at the grocery store and fed as finger food to most babies seven months and older.
- Puree crab or lobster and offer it mixed with a vegetable puree that they already like.
- Make fish fingers with a variety of different fish species.
- Offer a quartered hard-boiled egg, scrambled eggs, or cooked yolks mixed with water to form a puree.
- Dilute ricotta and yogurt with water to form a puree.
- Purchase baby cereal that contains wheat flour or serve wholewheat pasta.
- Puree salmon or other fish.
- Use diluted tahini as a spread or add to hummus—sesame is not on the big eight list, but it is another known allergen that you should introduce early.

When and How To Introduce "Treat Foods"?

Desserts and other treat foods are sometimes used as a reward for good behavior because they are easy to give and highly motivational. This can easily turn into a negative relationship with food and goes against the practice of intuitive eating. It is important to use hugs, praise, and attention to reward behaviors that you like in your child. Be aware of how you offer "treat foods" to your child.

For the most part, sweets and desserts should be avoided entirely till twelve months of age and even longer if you choose.[1] However, look around; treats are everywhere and extremely difficult to completely avoid.

Every parent has a different idea of what a treat food is, but regardless of how strict or relaxed you want to be around sweets, it is your job to teach your kids healthy eating habits, not tell them what they can and can't have. In order to implement a healthy relationship with "treat foods," refrain from defining any food that you deem less healthy with words like "treat," "special," "comfort," or "reward food." Food is just-food. When your child asks for ice cream or cake, you don't have to say yes all the time, but you don't need to say no all the time either.

In order to foster healthy eating habits around "treat foods," implement these principles:[2]

1. Make dessert whatever you want it to be. Dessert means a lot of things to a lot of people, and your baby doesn't come out of the womb knowing what dessert is, so it is up to you to decide. It could be yogurt, dates, apples or homemade Popsicles. It doesn't always have to mean ice cream, cake, and cookies.
2. Control the portion size and don't always make it a separate event from dinner. Feel free to include a small portion of dessert and serve it with the main meal. This reinforces the idea that dessert is just food and the same as all the other items on their plate.
3. When you have cookies in the house, everyone gets one regardless of whether they behaved or ate their dinner. Dessert is never a reward, and to help implement this, it can be helpful to plan the nights that dessert will be offered ahead of time and stick to it.

Every parent can do BLW if they utilize all the tips above. It might take a little bit more planning on your end, but it can get you into the habit of cooking and preparing healthy and hearty meals from the beginning.

Chapter 8
Easy Three-Ingredient Recipes

While I highly recommend sticking to your favorite adult recipes and modifying them to be BLW approved, I also understand that you might want some staple recipes that can be your go-to meals initially. There are thousands of BLW recipes on the Internet, and if you're going to do just one thing to make BLW easier and stress-free, ditch the fancy recipes!

All the recipes below are three ingredients or less and are appropriate for children six months and older. Feel free to double the recipe if you want lots of leftovers to freeze, and halve the recipe if you want only a small amount for maybe one or two meals.

Baby Pancakes

Yields: 20 pancakes

Supplies: Mixing bowl, frying pan, and fork.

Ingredients:

- 2 medium ripe bananas
- 2 large eggs
- 4 tbsp flour

Instructions:

1. Heat frying pan to medium/low heat
2. Mash bananas in a bowl with a fork
3. Add egg and flour
4. Mix until batter forms a runny consistency
5. Oil pan with coconut oil or your preferred oil
6. Drop 1 tbsp of batter at a time onto the griddle
7. Cook for approximately 1-3 minutes on each side or until you see bubbles forming on the pancake and the bottom is slightly brown
8. Let cool and cut into strips

Options:

- Substitute one banana with 3/4 cup sweet potato or pumpkin
- Substitute flour with oat flour, spelt flour, rice flour, buckwheat flour, or any other preferred flour
- Add ⅓ cup of grated carrot, apple, zucchini, mashed berries, or shredded coconut
- Add ½ tsp of cinnamon, cloves, vanilla, or nutmeg

*Inspired by Michele Olivier from Baby Foodie*1

French Toast

Yields: 9-12 strips

Supplies: Mixing bowl, frying pan

Ingredients:

- 3 pieces wholegrain toast (low salt/no salt)
- 2 eggs
- 1/4 cup breast milk or formula (cow's milk can be used in a pinch)

Instructions:

1. Heat frying pan to medium heat
2. Whisk eggs and milk together with a fork
3. Oil pan
4. Place bread in egg mixture and coat on each side
5. Cook for 2-3 minutes on each side
6. Remove and cut into strips the size of 1-2 adult fingers

Options:

- Add 1/2 tsp ginger, vanilla, cinnamon, or nutmeg to the egg mixture

Egg Muffins

Yields: 12 muffins

Supplies: Mixing bowl, 12-hole muffin pan

Ingredients:

- 7 eggs
- 1 1/2 cup steamed vegetables, minced by hand or in a food processor
- 1 cup cheese

Instructions:

1. Preheat oven to 375° F
2. Oil muffin tin with butter or oil of choice
3. Mix all ingredients together
4. Pour into muffin tin, filling each cup halfway
5. Cook for 12-15 minutes or until eggs are fully set
6. Let cool and serve whole

Optional vegetable and cheese combos:

- Spinach and feta
- Eggplant and Parmesan
- Broccoli and cheddar
- Tomato and mozzarella
- Kale and provolone
- Green onions and cream cheese
- Radish and goat cheese
- Bell pepper and Swiss cheese

*Inspired by Heather from Fit Mama Real Food*2

Popsicles

Yields: 12 Popsicles

Supplies: Mini Popsicle molds, blender

Ingredients:

- 1 cup full-fat Greek yogurt
- 1⅓ cups fruit (fresh or frozen)
- Half a banana

Instructions:

1. Blend all ingredients together
2. Pour into Popsicle molds
3. Freeze for 3-5 hours
4. Run the outside of the mold under warm water to easily remove the Popsicle

Optional fruits:

- Strawberry
- Blueberry
- Peach
- Pineapple
- Raspberry
- Blackberry
- Cherry
- Mango

Inspired by Michele Olivier from Baby Foodie[3]

Potato Fritters

Yields: 10-12 fritters

Supplies: Mixing bowl, frying pan, grater

Ingredients:

- 3 cups grated potato
- 2 egg
- 1/2 cup cheese

Instructions:

1. Grate potato
2. Heat frying pan to medium heat
3. Mix grated potato, egg, and cheese in a bowl
4. Oil pan with coconut oil or your preferred oil
5. Spoon 2 tsp of batter into the frying pan at a time
6. Cook for 2 minutes on each side or until brown and crispy
7. Let cool and cut in strips

Optional:

- Substitute potato with sweet potato or yams
- Add ½ tsp of cumin, garlic, or onion

Finger Meatballs

Yields: 12 meatballs

Supplies: mixing bowl, cookie sheet

Ingredients:

- 1 egg
- 1 lb. ground beef, chicken, or pork
- ⅓ cup baby oats

Instructions:

1. Preheat oven to 400° F
2. Mix all ingredients together in a bowl
3. Form into long meatballs the size of an adult's finger
4. Bake for 15 minutes or until internal temperature reaches 160° F

Options:

- Substitute baby oats with chickpea flour, oat flour, or breadcrumbs
- Add ¼ cup grated apple, carrot, cheese, or minced onion
- Add 1 tsp garlic, thyme, oregano, or parsley

Finger Fish Cakes

Yields: 20 cakes

Supplies: Mixing bowl, food processor, frying pan

Ingredients:

- ½ cup breadcrumbs
- 15 oz fresh fish or 3 small cans of tuna or salmon
- 2 eggs

Instructions:

1. Heat frying pan to medium heat or preheat oven to 350° F
2. Add fish, eggs, and breadcrumbs to a bowl and mix well until a paste forms
3. Shape batter into long strips the size of an adult's finger
4. Oil pan with coconut oil or your preferred oil
5. Cook in frying pan for 2-4 minutes per side or bake for 15 minutes on the top rack

Optional:

- Add to food processor 1-2 tbsp chopped onion
- Add ½ tsp paprika, ¼ tsp black pepper, or any other spice of choice

*Inspired by Aileen Blunder from Baby-Led Feeding*4

Tofu Strips

Yields: 16-20 strips

Supplies: Cookie sheet, frying pan

Ingredients:

- 1 block extra-firm organic tofu
- 1-2 tbsp oil

Instructions:

1. Drain excess water out of tofu by placing a layer of paper towels on the top and bottom and putting something heavy on top of the block like a can of soup
2. Let the tofu sit for 30 minutes or until the paper towel stops absorbing moisture
3. Cut tofu into strips the size of an adult finger
4. Heat frying pan to medium heat and coat with oil
5. Place strips in pan and cook on each side for roughly 1-2 minutes.

Optional:

- Prior to cooking, coat tofu with arrowroot powder or corn starch for a crispy texture
- Add garlic, cumin, or oregano to add flavor

Inspired by Michele Olivier from Baby Foodie5

Liver Pate

Yields: 1 cup pate

Supplies: Food processor, frying pan

Ingredients:

- 1/2 lb. chicken livers
- 1/2 water
- 2 tbsp butter

Instructions:

1. Add livers to a frying pan and cook until internal temperature reaches 165° F (they should be firm and completely brown in the center)
2. Place cooked livers in a food processor with water and butter, blend until smooth
3. Add more water or butter for a smoother consistency
4. Spread on toast or pita bread or spoon-feed

Options:

- Add 1/4 cup onion to frying pan with liver
- Replace water with breast milk
- Add 1/4 cup cooked carrots, sweet potato, cauliflower, or apple to food processor

Hummus

Yields: 2 cups hummus

Supplies: Food processor

Ingredients:

- 1 can chickpeas
- 1/3 cup tahini
- 1 tbsp lemon juice (omit if under eight months due to acid)

Instructions:

1. Strain chickpeas and reserve the liquid
2. Add chickpeas to a food processor and blend
3. Add tahini and blend
4. Add lemon juice and blend
5. Add 1 tbsp of reserved liquid at a time until you get the consistency of applesauce. I usually use half of the reserved liquid for this.

Optional:

- Add ¼ tsp thyme, garlic, cumin
- Add 1 Tbsp olive oil
- Add 1-3 drops sesame oil

*Inspired by Shane and Simple*6

Pasta

Ingredients:

- Penne, bowtie, fusilli, or large shells

Instructions: Cook pasta as per package instructions and mix with a sauce of choice

Cheese Sauce

- 1/2 cup heavy cream
- 1 cup shredded cheddar cheese
- 1/3 cup shredded Parmesan

Instructions: In a saucepan, heat cream till warm, then add cheese, and stir until melted

Avocado Cream Sauce

- 1 medium avocado
- 1 tsp lemon juice
- Pinch garlic powder

Instructions: Place all ingredients in a food processor and blend until smooth

Sweet Potato Sauce

- 1 large tomato
- 1 medium sweet potato cooked
- Pinch of garlic

Instructions: Place all ingredients in a food processor and blend until smooth

Butter Sauce

- ¼ cup butter
- 2 tbsp nutritional yeast

- ½ tsp parsley

Instructions: Mix melted butter with nutritional yeast and parsley

Tomato Sauce

- Homemade or store-bought tomato sauce (no added sugar)

Pesto

- 2 cups basil
- ⅓ cup pine nuts
- ⅔ cup olive oil

Instructions: Place all ingredients in a food processor and blend until smooth

Pulled Pork

Yields: 3 lb. shredded meat

Supplies: Instapot

Ingredients:

- 4 lb. pork shoulder or pork butt
- 1 medium sweet onion
- 2 cups no-salt vegetable broth or water

Instructions:

1. Place pork in the Instapot
2. Add broth or water and scatter onions around and on top of the pork
3. Secure lid
4. Cook for 90 minutes and allow pressure to release naturally
5. Remove pork and let rest for 10-20 minutes
6. Shred or cut into chunks against the grain

Optional:

- Add 1 tbsp apple cider vinegar
- Replace 1 cup broth/water with unsweetened applesauce

*Inspired by Kelli from Hungry Hobby*7

Chicken Drumsticks

Yields: 6 drumsticks

Supplies: Baking sheet

Ingredients:

- 6 chicken drumsticks
- Seasoning: pepper, garlic, basil or any other herb

Instructions:

1. Preheat oven to 375° F
2. Pat chicken legs dry with a paper towel
3. Season legs with preferred seasoning
4. Bake for 20 minutes, turn, and cook for another 10-15 minutes or until internal temperature reaches 165° F
5. Remove from oven, let cool
6. Remove skin and serve whole

Peanut Butter Cookies

Yields: 16-18 cookies

Supplies: Mixing bowl, cookie sheet

Ingredients:

- 2 cup rolled oats or 1 cup rolled oats and ¾ cup baby oats
- 4 tbsp peanut butter
- 4 ripe medium bananas

Instructions:

1. Preheat oven to 350° F
2. Mash ripe bananas
3. Mix in peanut butter and 1 cup rolled oats
4. Blend 1 cup rolled oats into a powder or use ¾ cup baby oats, add to bowl and mix
5. Scoop tbsps of mix onto a parchment paper-lined baking sheet
6. Flatten with a fork
7. Bake for 25-30 minutes. Cookies will be soft when taken out of the oven and will need to cool to firm up.

Options:

- Sub 1 tbsp of peanut butter with molasses
- Add: 1 tsp vanilla, cinnamon, nutmeg, or allspice
- Add ¼ cup shredded coconut or carrots

Inspired by Min from MJ & Hungryman8

Baby Cake

Yields: 9-inch cake

Supplies: Mixing bowl, 9-inch cake pan (23 cm)

Ingredients

- 3 eggs
- 2 cups yogurt
- 1 ¼ cup self-rising flour (or 1 ¼ cup flour and 1 ½ tsp baking powder)

Instructions:

1. Preheat oven to 400° F
2. Combine all ingredients and mix well
3. Pour into a pre-greased 9-inch round pan
4. Cover with aluminum foil and bake on middle rack for 20 minutes
5. Remove foil, poke the top with a fork multiple times, and cook for another 20-25 minutes

Options:

- Replace yogurt with sour cream
- Add ½ cup shredded carrots or raisins
- Add 1 tsp cinnamon, ginger, nutmeg, or lemon/orange zest

Inspired by Loana from Weaningful9

Oatmeal Fingers:

Yields: 10 fingers

Supplies: Baking pan 8x8

Ingredients:

- 1 ¼ cup oats
- 1 ¼ cup milk (coconut, oat, almond, soy)
- 1 tsp cinnamon

Instructions:

1. Preheat oven to 375° F
2. Mix all ingredients together and let sit for 5 minutes
3. Spread mixture into an 8x8 pan
4. Bake for 20 minutes
5. Cool and slice into strips

Options:

- Add grated carrots or apple
- Add halved blueberries or raspberries
- Replace cinnamon with nutmeg or ginger
- Can also be done in the microwave; cook for 2 minutes and 30 seconds on high till firm

*Inspired by Amy from Healthy Little Foodie*10

Chapter 9
Healthy Meal Plans & Schedules

As a first-time parent or if you're new to BLW, you might be curious about what a typical day should look like when you start weaning. I have provided a rough guideline below, including how your schedule will change as your infant becomes better at eating. Keep in mind that your baby will still be napping, nursing, or drinking from a bottle, and also trying purees or solids.

It is unlikely that your baby will follow any schedule exactly, but the below schedules will give you a basic idea. Your baby's progress with solid food will have ups and downs throughout the first six months. As their skills advance with eating solid food, their breast/bottle feeding sessions will gradually decrease as they become less hungry. This should be a slow and natural process, so let your baby guide you.

6-7 Months

- Roughly 4-6 nursing or bottle-feeding sessions per day (volume should stay the same)
- 3 naps
- 1 BLW/puree in the morning roughly 45-90 minutes after nursing or bottle-feeding

- 1 BLW/puree feeding in the evening, 45-90 minutes after nursing or bottle-feeding
- 1-4 solid foods per meal
- Portions should be roughy the same size for every meal[1]

Sample Schedule

7:00—breast or bottle feed

8:00—solids or purees

9:00-11:00—nap

11:00—breast or bottle feed

12:30-14:30—nap

14:30—breast or bottle feed

16:00-16:45—nap

16:45—breast or bottle feed

17:45—solids or purees

18:45—breast or bottle feed

19:00—bed

7-9 Months

- The volume of solid food starts to increase.
- Nursing sessions decrease only slightly, roughly three nursing or bottle-feeding sessions per day. Let this happen naturally and look for cues.
- 2 naps
- 3 BLW/purees per day, 45-90 minutes after nursing or bottle feeding. Your baby might not be eating during all meals, but still exploring and playing.[2]

10-12 Months

- The volume of solid food continues to increase.

- Nurse or bottle-feed only in the morning and before bed. These two feedings will typically be the last to go.
- BLW meal for breakfast, lunch, dinner, and snacks, grazing all day is okay.[3]

First Week Meal Plan for Baby-Led Weaning

Not sure how to get started and what to offer first? Don't worry; below, I have put together exactly what your first week of baby-led weaning can look like. Remember, you only need to offer single foods to start with. These will be easier to explore and be less overwhelming. It is best to start slow and add new foods alongside the ones your child is already familiar with. Try to offer one to two meals a day initially, typically one in the morning and one toward the evening, roughly 45-90 minutes after a feed.

All meals have been reviewed by a registered pediatric dietitian to ensure proper nutrition.

Day 1:

Meal 1: 1 steamed broccoli floret (vegetable/iron)

Meal 2: 1 egg omelet cut into strips (protein/iron)

Note: You are introducing the first potential allergen (egg), so pay attention to any allergy signs.

Day 2:

Meal 1: 1 Steamed broccoli floret (vegetable/iron) + 1 sweet potato fry (starch)

Meal 2: 1 egg omelet cut into strips (protein/iron) + 1 avocado spear (fat)

Day 3:

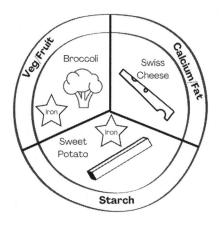

Meal 1: 1 steamed broccoli floret (vegetable/iron) + 1 sweet potato fry (starch) + 1 Swiss cheese strip (calcium/fat)

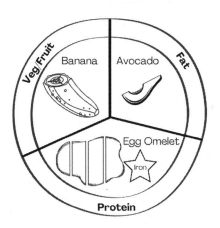

Meal 2: 1 egg omelet cut into strips (protein/iron) + 1 avocado spear (fat) + ½ banana (fruit)

Day 4:

Meal 1: 2 steamed carrot spears (vegetable) + 1 wholegrain toast strip (starch/iron) + 1 Swiss cheese strip (calcium/fat)

Meal 2: 1 steak strip (protein/iron) + 1 avocado spear (fat) + 1 steamed apple wedge — skin removed (fruit)

Note: You are introducing another potential allergen (wheat), so pay attention to any allergy signs.

Day 5:

Meal 1: 2 steamed carrot spears (vegetable) + 1 wholegrain toast strip (starch/iron) + 1/4 cup plain full fat yogurt (calcium/fat)

Meal 2: 1 steak strip (protein/iron) + 1 avocado spear (fat) + 1 steamed apple wedge — skin removed (fruit)

Day 6 and beyond:

As you complete your first week and continue with BLW, choose new foods from each of the five categories: protein, starch, fat, calcium, and fruits/vegetables. Continue providing healthy, balanced meals, focus on iron-rich foods, and introduce the eight most common allergens as you rotate new foods. Every meal should contain roughly three to four foods. Try to keep at least some foods in each meal foods that they have already tried before and are familiar with.

Keep in mind that a lot of the BLW meals you see online have huge portions. In the beginning and for the first few months, your baby will only need 1-2 tablespoons of food per day. It is very easy to give your child way too much food and then quickly feel like a failure when they barely eat anything.

To start with, only offer one to two slices of each food and add more as needed until they show signs of being done. Once their skills develop and they can successfully eat a quantity of food, try to give them everything you think they might eat in a meal at the start. It is still okay if they eat less or more, but this allows them to prepare for the meal visually.

It is also important to note that your baby has no idea what breakfast, lunch, or dinner is. Eggs for dinner, spaghetti for breakfast, and pancakes for lunch are all normal. Do not feel limited to only serving breakfast foods for breakfast and so on.

Your baby also does not know what foods go with what. There is a high likelihood that they will dip meat in diluted peanut butter, cucumber in applesauce, and many other weird food combinations that you wouldn't want to try yourself. Let them explore and figure out on their own what they like combined. They might even discover something new.

Meals can change from day to day and week to week as their enthusiasm and willingness to explore ebbs and flows. There will be some meals where they only take one bite and others where they explore the entire plate as they regulate their own appetite. It is also unlikely that you will see improvement every day, but instead, you will notice times of rapid improvement and even some instances of decline. It's all just part of the ride.

Beginner Meal Plan/Ideas

When you start BLW, it is best to offer roughly two meals a day as you and your baby learn together what will work for your family. Remember, this is a time for experimentation and trial. Most of the food won't make it into your baby's stomach. Your only goal should be to expose them to as many foods as possible. If you find your baby can eat more or less than the below meals, then adjust accordingly; they are just a starting point for you to work from.

All meals have been reviewed by a registered pediatric dietitian to ensure proper nutrition.

Idea #1

Breakfast

- 1 egg omelet cut into strips cooked in healthy oil (protein/fat/iron)
- 1 sweet potato fry (starch)
- 1 peach spear — skin removed (fruit)
- 1 Swiss cheese stick (calcium/fat)

Dinner

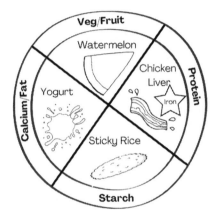

- ¼ cup yogurt (calcium/fat)
- 1 chicken liver strip (protein/iron)
- 1 watermelon slice — large triangle shape (fruit)
- 1 sticky rice finger (starch)

Optional: Replace one meal with purees and experiment with baby-led spoon-feeding. Example: pumpkin puree, raisin puree, carrot puree, avocado puree, or Stage 1 store-bought puree.

Idea #2

Lunch

- 1 chicken/steak strip (protein/iron)
- 2 pita strips (starch)
- 1 mozzarella cheese strip (calcium/fat)

Dinner

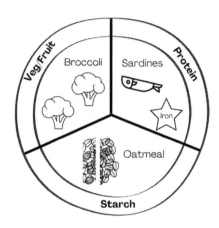

- 1 can sardines (protein/iron)
- 2 broccoli florets (vegetable/iron)
- 2 oatmeal fingers — see recipe (starch)

Optional: Replace one meal with purees and experiment with baby-led spoon-feeding. Example: yogurt or peanut butter mixed with soy milk, water, formula, or breast milk.

Idea #3

Breakfast

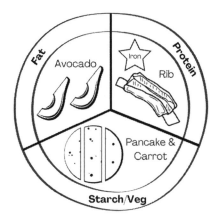

- 1 rib (protein/iron)
- 2 avocado slices (fat)
- 1 baby pancake with grated carrots — see recipe
  (starch/vegetable)

Lunch

- 2 french toast strips — see recipe (starch/protein/iron)
- 2 pear spears (fruit)

Dinner

- 1 zucchini spear (vegetable)
- 2 tofu strips (protein/iron)
- 2 butternut squash spears with coconut oil (starch/fat)
- 1 cheddar cheese strip (calcium/fat)

Optional: replace one meal with purees and experiment with baby-led spoon-feeding. Example: applesauce, mashed black beans, baby oatmeal, ricotta cheese, or meat puree

Intermediate Meal Plan/Ideas

As your child's skills improve, they will become ready for three meals a day. Keep in mind, the quantity you are offering at each meal doesn't necessarily increase, because more of the food is actually making it into your child's stomach at this point, instead of going on the floor or the baby.

Idea #1

Breakfast

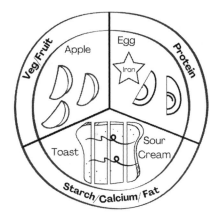

- 4 toast strips with sour cream (starch/fat/calcium)
- 2 quarters of a hard-boiled egg (protein/iron)
- 3 cooked apple wedges, skin removed, sprinkled with hemp hearts (fruit/iron)

Lunch

- Lobster or crab puree with cooked spinach (protein/iron)
- Juicy mango pit (fruit)

Dinner

- 2 lamb strips (protein/iron)
- ½ cup lentil pasta with cheese sauce (starch/protein/calcium/fat)
- 2 portabella strips (vegetable)

Idea #2

Breakfast

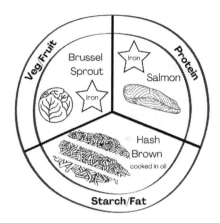

- 2 oz salmon (protein/iron)
- 3 hash brown strips cooked in healthy oil (starch/fat)
- 1 steamed Brussels sprout (vegetable)

Lunch

- 1 green onion (vegetable)
- 4 toast strips with diluted tahini (starch/protein/iron)
- 3 avocado spears (fat)

Dinner

- 1 turkey meatball finger (protein/iron)
- ¼ cup ricotta (calcium/fat)
- 3 polenta strips (starch)

Idea #3

Breakfast

- 1 finger fish cake — see recipe (protein/iron)
- ½ banana (fruit)
- ¼ cup yogurt (fat/calcium)
- 2 red pepper slices for sucking (vegetable)

Lunch

- 1 English muffin with diluted peanut butter (starch/fat)
- 2 cauliflower florets (vegetable)
- ½ cup mashed kidney beans (protein/iron)

Dinner

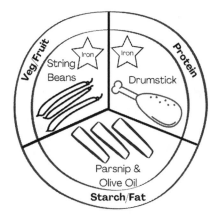

- 3 large green beans (vegetable/iron)
- 3 parsnip spears — drizzle with olive oil (starch/fat)
- 1 chicken drumstick (protein/iron)

Advanced Meal Plan/Ideas

Idea #1

Breakfast.

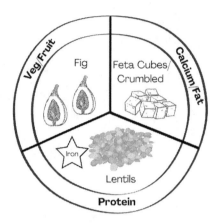

- 1 fig — halved (fruit)
- ¼ cup feta crumbled or cut in cubes(calcium/fat)
- ½ cup lentils (protein/iron)

Lunch

- ½ cup squished black beans with grated cheddar cheese (protein/iron/calcium)
- 3 tomato slices (vegetable)
- 1 kiwi cut into wedges (fruit)

Dinner

- ½ cup pulled pork (protein/iron)
- 8 white potato cubes (starch)
- 2 bok choy leaves (vegetable)

Idea #2:

Breakfast

- 1 cup oatmeal with shredded carrot, hemp seeds, molasses, butter, and spices (starch/vegetable/fat/iron)

Lunch

- 2 shrimps sliced lengthwise (protein/iron)
- 3 spears asparagus cooked in oil (vegetable/fat)
- ¼ cup mascarpone for dipping (calcium/fat)

Dinner

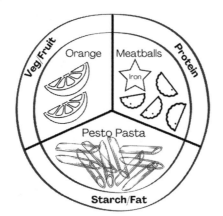

- 1 cup penne pasta with pesto (starch/fat)
- 2 bison meatballs, cut in half (protein/iron)
- 2 orange wedges (fruit)

Idea #3

Breakfast

- 1 egg muffin with blended spinach and broccoli (protein/iron/vegetable)
- 8 ripe pear cubes (fruit)

Lunch

- 2 oz shredded chicken (protein/iron)
- 8 melon cubes (fruit)
- ¼ cup cottage cheese (calcium)

Dinner

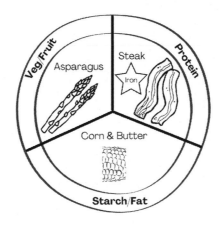

- 2-inch (5 cm) corn on the cob round with butter (starch/fat)
- 2 asparagus spears (vegetable)
- 2 steak strips (protein/iron)

Snack Ideas

At the beginning of weaning, from six to twelve months, you want to limit snacks as much as possible. Babies have an amazing ability to be intuitive eaters and will only eat when they are hungry. Offering snacks when they should be getting the majority of their nutrients and calories from breast milk or formula can disrupt their growth and nutrition.

When your baby turns one, you will quickly notice that they have an increased desire to snack as their consumption of breast milk or formula is eliminated or dramatically reduced.

Store-bought snacks like pouches and teething crackers can be a great option in a pinch, but aren't something you want to become reliant on all the time. There are many snacks you can make at home that are quick and full of nutrition.

Here are some of my favorites:

- Vegetable sticks (carrot, cucumber, bell pepper, jicama)
- Fruit (banana, peach, pear, strawberries, blueberries)
- Any homemade muffin (freeze and defrost when needed)
- Any homemade cookie (freeze and defrost when needed)
- Any homemade patty (freeze and defrost when needed)
- Pancakes (freeze and defrost when needed)
- Avocado on toast
- Peanut butter on rice cakes
- Cubed cheese
- Mozzarella sticks
- Egg muffins (freeze and defrost when needed)
- Boiled Egg

Chapter 10
Common Mistakes and Questions

When it comes to feeding our babies, we all make mistakes and have questions. Wondering if you are doing the right thing is normal. Whether it is your first child or your sixth, each baby behaves and responds differently to food. Here are some of the common misunderstandings and answers to questions that will help you along your journey.

My child is coughing, choking, and has difficulty breathing when eating purees. Is this normal?

Gagging and sometimes choking in the initial days of weaning can be normal, but if you see that your baby is really struggling after a few attempts, it is a good idea to meet with a speech-language pathologist with experience in feeding therapy.

If your child has difficulty with purees, you do not want to start BLW until these difficulties are addressed and they can safely and effectively consume purees.

While feeding purees, my baby wants to suck on the spoon and gets upset when we remove it.

Although this might seem like a waste of time when you would like them to be eating, there are skills that the child is improving by doing this. First and foremost, they are learning how to elevate and depress the tongue. This skill will enhance their ability to control food in their mouth and more effectively chew and swallow.[1]

This behavior is also common with babies new to weaning as they have gotten really good at sucking from the breast or bottle and are eager to try their skills on other objects. As they gain control of their upper lip and can remove food from the spoon, this behavior should diminish.

My baby only plays with solid food, so I feed purees after to ensure they get all their nutrient requirements.

It is not a good idea to offer purees after a BLW meal, regardless of how much they eat. If this becomes a habit, the baby expects to always get purees after playing with their solid food, and the incentive of learning how to eat is removed.[2] If you want to receive the various benefits of BLW, you want to encourage them to learn how to eat.

You also do not need to be concerned with your baby getting enough calories or nutrients from a meal. As long as you continue to breastfeed or bottle-feed, food can be playtime for the first few weeks to months. Even from nine to twelve months, they only need to eat a few tablespoons of food per day.[3] Try to get past the common notion that babies need to be eating or something must be wrong. Your child intuitively knows how to eat enough for their current needs.

Should I only use purees if I don't want my baby to gag or choke?

The gag reflex is different in all babies. Sadly, gagging happens with pureed food, solid food, and even sometimes with formula or breast milk. You cannot escape gagging episodes by just feeding purees.

Although spoon-fed babies gag less initially, they gag more as they get older.

The 2016 Bliss Study found that babies usually fed purees gag less at six months but more at eight months and older.[4] This is because the baby's gag reflex is less sensitive by eight months and allows foods to make it closer to the throat even though they have not had as much experience as a baby eating finger foods. A purely spoon-fed baby will have less advanced skills and a high likelihood of gagging as they begin solid foods at an older age.

Babies who follow BLW are busy practicing eating solid food, and by the time the gag reflex decreases, they are experts in chewing and swallowing solid food. This is why it is recommended to include both purees and solids in a child's diet as long as they are developmentally ready.

My baby pushes out anything that she puts in her mouth. What should I do?

This is a very common response if your child is new to weaning. They likely haven't lost their tongue-thrust reflex or don't have enough lip control to keep food in their mouth. If the tongue-thrust reflex is still very active, it pushes the tongue forward when the mouth is stimulated.[5]

It is one of the many ways that Mother Nature ensures that your baby is safe and doesn't swallow something they aren't supposed to at a young age. If this is the case, keep offering food to explore and play with without expecting them to eat.

On the other hand, if they can hold food in their mouth for a few seconds before it falls out, it is more likely they haven't developed the ability to lift and curl their lips while eating. Over time, as more food touches the inside mouth and they work their lip and jaw muscles, they will quickly learn how to keep food inside.

What if I have been spoon-feeding my child for months? Can I do baby-led weaning?

Absolutely! In order to ease into it, start by alternating between solid foods and purees for different meals. You can even try offering solid food that you have previously offered in a puree form. Since your child is already familiar with the taste, they will likely be more accepting.

It is good to introduce solids at the earliest age possible once they reach six months and are developmentally ready. Recent research has concluded that if babies aren't fed lumpy food by nine months, their risk of feeding difficulties later in life increases.[6]

Will using purees ruin the baby-led weaning process and make it more dangerous?

There is no scientific proof that using purees and BLW for different meals during weaning is dangerous. Many parents have fantastic success with combo feeding. Just remember to avoid offering purees and solids combined into the same food, like soup, in the beginning. Separating solids from liquids is an advanced skill.

I introduced my baby to avocado, and they didn't like it. Should I keep offering it?

Although you might be convinced your baby doesn't like a particular food, this is not always the case. A facial expression or not eating a specific food does not necessarily mean they don't like it. It might just be a new flavor or too challenging for them at this time. It is vital to keep introducing new food to your baby during the weaning process, regardless of their reaction.

If you find your child doesn't touch or eat a particular food, keep exposing it to them. Eventually, they are going to try it and probably like it too. However, it can take as many as 8-20 tries before a baby accepts a new food. Forestell and Menella confirmed in their research that when they gave babies green beans to eat for eight days in a row, they overcame their dislike and ate three times the number of green beans they were eating on day one.[7] Keep trying and never give up on a food.

I have introduced solids, and my baby doesn't seem interested at all. What should I do?

Each baby has a different developmental pattern and becomes ready at different times. If the baby is not interested in the solid foods you have offered, take a break for a few days and try again. When you re-introduce solid food, ensure that there are minimal distractions and both the parent and baby are happy.

You can also offer a pre-loaded spoon with a puree; they might have more interest in this than solid food. If they continue to resist and show no interest in solid food after eight months old, it would be best to talk to a health care professional.

My baby is not eating enough. What should I do?

The amount of food a baby needs changes dramatically due to their age, weight, genetics, and activity level. It is best to trust that your baby is getting what they need regardless of what your other children or friends' babies are eating.

Your baby also might not eat as much when a stressful life change occurs. Babies can be sensitive to new people, new environments, and other changes in the household. Eating a lot of food should never be considered a success. Instead, observe how your child's eating habits change, but never label them as good or bad.

What if my baby is sick with a cold, teething, or has any other short-term illness?

Continue to offer food in the same manner, but be aware that their food consumption might decrease dramatically when they don't feel well. If they are completely uninterested in food, feel free to offer more breast milk or formula than usual and wait to offer solid foods until they feel better.

What if my baby has a history of acid reflux?

Acid reflux is very common in babies and it typically goes away over time as their digestive tract grows and strengthens. There are a lot of symptoms that could indicate your baby is suffering from acid reflux, but the most common are spitting up, vomiting, refusal to eat, wet burps, and chest pain. It is important to talk to your doctor if you suspect your infant might be suffering from acid reflux. Medication can be prescribed, and your doctor might recommend starting weaning earlier.

Weaning a baby with acid reflux will be similar to traditional weaning, with a few key adjustments. First, it is essential to give plenty of time for breast milk or formula to be digested before offering purees or solid food; ensure that purees or solid food are offered at least 1-2 hours after a feed. Secondly, it is imperative to take things slowly. Allow extra time for each meal, and don't rush. A reflux baby won't eat a lot per meal, and you want to allow plenty of time for the food to settle in their stomach.

Babies with acid reflux normally do very well on smooth purees, non-acidic fruit, and bland foods like chicken, eggs, or oatmeal. Avoid oranges, tomatoes, apples, peppers, spicy foods, extra fatty foods, and anything with milk protein. You do not have to be extra cautious about the Big 8 allergens; they will not worsen symptoms unless your child is allergic to one.

Be aware that your weaning journey might move more slowly than you would have anticipated because you will need to take your time with introducing new textures and foods. Try offering a new food every 3-4 days in order to give your baby's digestive tract plenty of time to acclimatize.

It can also be difficult to gauge the hunger and satiety cues of a baby with acid reflux, so baby-led weaning is a great solution, because it gives them complete control over what goes into their mouth. With spoon-feeding, you always have the risk of putting food in your baby's mouth when they don't want it and this makes them feel sicker and more uncomfortable.

It is important to find out what works for you and your baby. Remember, even if your baby's reflux is too severe for them to eat any finger foods, they will still improve their skills just by playing with the food.

My baby makes faces while eating. What does this mean?

Babies can be overly expressive while eating, wrinkling their noses, raising the upper lip, moving their brows, and squinting. Sometimes it is adorable and other times, you're confused and worried. Although they might be showing signs of discomfort, these expressions can indicate anything. Sometimes, faces mean nothing at all.[8] Never assume that a baby dislikes a food purely based on their expression.

When should I be alarmed by gagging?

Gagging naturally protects the baby from choking and is your biggest friend during this journey. Your child will likely gag a lot in the beginning, but if they continue to gag after they have passed the initial learning process of figuring out how to eat, then ask yourself these three questions.[9]

1. Is your baby upset after gagging? They might cry, vomit, or throw a tantrum.
2. Does your baby vomit a lot during mealtimes and even on an empty stomach?
3. After one to two months of weaning, is your child still gagging at most meals?

If you answered yes to any of the questions above, it would be best to speak to a healthcare professional.

I'm worried about my baby getting enough nutrition. Nothing gets eaten.

Babies get everything except iron from breast milk or formula up until their first birthday. They will quickly learn how to eat and swallow more foods as they practice, but in the meantime, focus on providing good sources of iron. Try to include more iron-rich purees and foods like bean and meat purees, infant cereal, baby oatmeal, scrambled eggs, etc. To ensure maximum iron consumption, combine iron-rich foods with vitamin C.

If you are still worried, analyze your baby's food intake over a week rather than seeing the food intake during a day or meal. They are likely consuming more than you think. You can also gauge the amount consumed by looking at their poop. If you see changes, then it means they are swallowing at least some food. You might even see particles of food in their poop. Give it time and trust that your baby will figure it out. In the meantime, view food as a time for exploration and learning.

Some days my child rejects spoon-feeding, some days self-feeding, and some days doesn't want to eat at all.

Weaning is a roller coaster instead of a ski lift. Just as adults' appetites change and fluctuate, babies' do too. It is perfectly normal for them to change their eating preferences, and your only job is to follow your child's cues. Babies will figure out how to eat over time, so try to be flexible and refrain from labeling anything as good or bad.

Everyone is telling me different things when it comes to weaning, and they all contradict one another. Who should I believe?

It can be very overwhelming, but my motto is "The parents always know best." If any foods make you nervous or you find that your child gags on them, remove them from their diet for a while. Always trust your gut. Over time, their skills will improve, and they will handle these foods better. As long as you follow the basic guidelines for safety, feel free to modify spoon-feeding or baby-led weaning so it works for your family.

Am I Feeding My Baby Way Too Much Salt or Sugar Without Realizing It?

Food is never bland to babies. It is new, different, and bursting with unique flavors. It is better not to add extra salt to any food. Babies' kidneys are not developed enough to deal with high quantities of salt. Babies under one year should have less than 0.4 g of sodium in a day. Many whole foods contain salt, e.g. beets, celery, carrots, and there is also a decent amount in breast milk.[10] Extra salt is never needed in your child's diet.

Sadly, a lot of sodium is contained in processed and packaged foods available in stores, and these are a big no-no for infants.

Here is a list of things that may have hidden salt in them:

- Bread
- Gravy
- Smoked fish
- Cheese
- Nut butter
- Olives
- Bacon and ham
- Cured meats and deli meats
- Stock cubes

Sugar is another ingredient that can be hidden in many foods. Although a moderate amount of fruit and other sources that naturally contain sugar are okay to include in your child's diet, added sugar should be avoided.

These foods can have hidden sugars:

- Purees—Always look at the ingredients before buying ready-to-eat purees

- Yogurt—Avoid fruit-flavored yogurt and choose plain instead
- Pasta sauce/ketchup—Opt for no added sugar
- Baked beans—Opt for no added sugar
- Bread—Choose sliced bread with no added sugar
- Canned fruits and vegetables—buy in water

Should I feed my baby juice?

Experts recommend that babies younger than twelve months should not be given juice as it contains little fiber and is just a concentrated form of sugar. Juices are found to add unnecessary calories, thus leading to extra weight and a lack of satiety.[11] If you find that your child is thirsty, a small amount of water is best in this situation. It is also important to ensure they are getting enough breast milk or formula.

However, if your baby has constipation, juices might provide the needed relief. It is best only to use them in this situation because they can cause diarrhea and GI distress if not needed.

How can I prevent my child from being fearful of new foods?

It is natural for a child aged two to six years to show fear of new foods, commonly known as neophobia. The fear of food or food refusal typically happens as a part of childhood development. They might dislike a portion of food that looks different or unfamiliar. If any food consists of a different texture, color, or smell and is not what they are used to, it is reason enough to reject it outright.[12]

For example, babies may refuse to eat bitter food, and unfortunately, many vegetables come under this category. They may push the plate away or start crying to avoid tasting the food.

The solution for this is to introduce your child to as many new foods as possible before twelve months. Introducing a new food every other day can be a challenging and exciting way to ensure they get exposed to as many foods as possible and eliminate any fear of food later on.

Rice is the main ingredient in my packaged baby food. I heard rice contains arsenic. Is it safe?

This is a widespread concern because baby cereal made with rice is one of the most popular foods purchased for infants. A small amount of arsenic or other metals like mercury or cadmium is always present in rice-containing food. The rice plant easily absorbs these unpleasant metallic substances from the soil it grows in. Brown rice has higher amounts of arsenic than white rice.[13]

However, this should not be a cause for concern as long as you are not overloading your baby with rice-containing food daily. If you are offering a balanced diet, an occasional rice-containing food once or twice a week is okay, but it should not become their primary diet. Instead, meals should focus on a variety of whole foods.

My baby isn't eating. How do I know if they have an oral aversion to solid food?

Babies love to put anything and everything in their mouths. This is their natural way of exploring the world. However, you might find that your child doesn't put anything in their mouth, including toys or food. This usually is one of the first signs that your baby might have an oral aversion to solids.

If your child still isn't willing to eat any solids by ten months old, it is likely an aversion to solid food. It is best to consult a healthcare professional to see if esophagus tightness, difficulties swallowing, or any other developmental delay is contributing to the aversion.[14]

My child just turned ten months old and won't try food anymore.

If your child has all of a sudden started throwing food on the floor instead of eating it, don't be alarmed. Teething is usually the initial trigger of this behavior. Due to the pain that comes with teething, it is normal for babies to reject all food. Although it is challenging to watch food being wasted, try to remain calm and refrain from giving the behavior much attention. Instead, keep offering smaller quantities of food so that less is wasted.

When should I stop feeding purees and only feed solid foods?

Typically, ten to twelve months is an excellent age to shift the diet to only solid foods. Babies need exposure to textures beyond purees, and solid food can also provide more variety of tastes. It is also likely at this age that your infant has developed the ability to eat and swallow more and more foods successfully, so they can eat foods very similar to yours.

Some parents might be reluctant to give up purees, but Ellyn Satter, an internationally recognized child feeding specialist, says it best: *"The goal of feeding your baby is to have him join you at the table... not for you to join him at the highchair."*[15]

Where can I learn more about infant CPR & first aid?

You can attend infant CPR classes online or at a local health facility. To find out more about infant CPR and first aid, refer to the resources below.

American Heart Association: Infant CPR Training Kits
https://cpr.heart.org/en/courses/infant-cpr-anytime-training-kits

American Red Cross: Child and Baby CPR
https://www.redcross.org/take-a-class/cpr/performing-cpr/child-baby-cpr

Heimlich Maneuver on an Infant
https://www.healthlinkbc.ca/illnesses-conditions/injuries/choking-rescue-procedure-heimlich-manoeuvre

Where Can I Learn More About Gagging vs. Choking?

The best way to educate yourself is to watch videos of what it looks like when a baby is gagging vs. choking. This will allow you to see the difference and help you to recognize it in your own child. Check out the videos below.

First aid and CPR for choking
https://youtu.be/gHZdBY-CkGw

What gagging looks like
https://www.youtube.com/watch?v=EZ6DEZbBx8A

Conclusion

Every pregnancy is different, every baby is different, every parent is different, and every decision is right.

Any new journey as a parent brings its own challenges and struggles, but by this point, your mind should be filled with ideas about how you can successfully wean your child. Whether you choose to implement a baby-led weaning approach, spoon-feeding approach, or combo method, you can eliminate picky eating, improve motor skills, and foster intuitive eating right from your baby's first bite. Whatever you decide, I firmly believe that every mom has a different opinion, but they are all right.

First, decide whether your child is ready to start weaning, and if you haven't had time to take an infant first aid class, get one booked. Pick a method that appeals to you and that you feel confident in. Next, take some time to familiarize yourself with the different foods you can offer and how they should be prepared. If you're short on time, prepare food ahead of time or purchase food that requires little to no prep. Even for parents who have decided to do only baby-led weaning, it can never hurt to have purees in the pantry.

For parents trying a combo method, practice baby-led spoon-feeding and notice the cues your baby gives you to indicate when they are hungry or full. Remember that your job is to provide what to eat, and it's your baby's job to decide on everything else.

Enjoy watching your baby explore new tastes and textures, and be open to changing and adapting as necessary. Every bite that your little one successfully takes will feel like an accomplishment for yourself and your baby, so enjoy the process and trust that you have all the right tools and knowledge to triumph.

Most of all, continue to practice responsive feeding as your baby becomes a toddler, a child, and an adolescent. Offer healthy whole foods and trust that they know when and how much to eat. The weaning journey is short and will be over before you know it, so have fun, learn, and explore as a family.

If you have any questions or you would like something clarified, feel free to email me at:

jocelyn@thefirst12months.com

I answer every single reader's emails.

If you feel like this book helped you through this difficult time, it would be wonderful if you could leave a review on Amazon. Reviews will help other parents realize that there is no one-size-fits-all with weaning and there are ways to make weaning stress-free and fun, even for the busy parent.

How to leave a review:

1. View *Spoons and Solids* on Amazon.
2. Scroll down to the customer reviews section
3. Click "Write a customer review" on the left-hand side.

Continuing Your Parenting Journey

"It takes a village to raise a baby."

There's a reason this African proverb gets thrown around so often. When parents have a community to support, encourage, and listen to them, raising a baby is so much easier. Parenting is a challenging experience, and having other parents there to answer your questions, provide new ideas, and let you know you are not alone is invaluable.

That's why we created the *Everything Babies Support Group*, so parents could get together to share ideas and learn from each other.

We regularly run giveaways, share wins from our readers, and answer all the awkward and difficult questions no one else wants to talk about.

It's 100% free and there are no requirements to join, except for the willingness to connect with, support, and learn from others.

You can join us on Facebook by going to:

www.thefirst12months.com/#facebook

Other Books by Jocelyn Goodwin

Available on Amazon & Audible

Help I'm A New Mom: Toddler Edition: A First-Time Mother's Guide to Positive Parenting, Gentle Discipline, and Practical Toddler Care

Help! I'm A New Mom: A First-Time Mother's Guide to Mastering
Newborn Care and Postpartum Recovery

Acknowledgments

Teamwork is always at the heart of any significant accomplishment. Although I get to interact with and receive all the kind messages from my amazing readers, I couldn't have done it without the people who helped make this book a reality.

First, I would like to thank Krista Jensema MS, RD, CSP, LD, CLC from Doherty Nutrition for her expertise and thorough review of all meal plans and nutritional components throughout the book.

I am grateful to Exxart for creating illustrations and giving the reader a visual representation.

I want to acknowledge our incredible editor, Jo Lavender, whose efforts made a good book into a great book.

I also would like to thank my family for their support, encouragement, and wisdom.

Lastly, thank you to everyone in the *Everything Babies Support Group* on Facebook. Your questions, input, and support are invaluable, and I am grateful for such a fantastic community of parents.

Much Love,

Jocelyn

Notes

1. What in the World Is Baby-Led Weaning?

1. D'Auria, E. (2018, May 3). *Baby-led weaning: what a systematic review of the literature adds on.* Italian Journal of Pediatrics. https://ijponline.biomedcentral.com/articles/10.1186/s13052-018-0487-8
2. Rachel Howcroft. (2013). *Weaned Upon A Time.* Stockholm University. https://citeseerx.ist.psu.edu/viewdoc/download?doi=10.1.1.461.9068&rep=rep1&type=pdf
3. Rachel Howcroft. (2013). *Weaned Upon A Time.* Stockholm University. https://citeseerx.ist.psu.edu/viewdoc/download?doi=10.1.1.461.9068&rep=rep1&type=pdf
4. Salas, D. (2019, October 16). *Are These the World's First Baby Bottles?* SAPIENS. https://www.sapiens.org/archaeology/neolithic-parenting-baby-bottles/
5. *Weaning through the ages: a parents' guide.* (2019, September 19). Bounty.Com. https://www.bounty.com/baby-0-to-12-months/weaning/ask-the-experts/weaning-through-the-ages
6. *Weaning through the ages: a parents' guide.* (2019, September 19). Bounty.Com. https://www.bounty.com/baby-0-to-12-months/weaning/ask-the-experts/weaning-through-the-ages
7. *Weaning through the ages: a parents' guide.* (2019, September 19). Bounty.Com. https://www.bounty.com/baby-0-to-12-months/weaning/ask-the-experts/weaning-through-the-ages
8. *Weaning through the ages: a parents' guide.* (2019, September 19). Bounty.Com. https://www.bounty.com/baby-0-to-12-months/weaning/ask-the-experts/weaning-through-the-ages
9. *Weaning through the ages: a parents' guide.* (2019, September 19). Bounty.Com. https://www.bounty.com/baby-0-to-12-months/weaning/ask-the-experts/weaning-through-the-ages
10. *Weaning through the ages: a parents' guide.* (2019, September 19). Bounty.Com. https://www.bounty.com/baby-0-to-12-months/weaning/ask-the-experts/weaning-through-the-ages
11. *Weaning through the ages: a parents' guide.* (2019, September 19). Bounty.Com. https://www.bounty.com/baby-0-to-12-months/weaning/ask-the-experts/weaning-through-the-ages
12. *Exclusive breastfeeding for six months best for babies everywhere.* (2011, January 15). World Health Organization. https://www.who.int/news/item/15-01-2011-exclusive-breastfeeding-for-six-months-best-for-babies-everywhere
13. Solid Starts. (2021, October 27). *The History of Baby Food - How Do We Feed Babies?* https://solidstarts.com/baby-led-weaning/history-of-baby-food/
14. Arsenault, A. (2017, March 2). *How Did Baby Food Become a Household Staple?* Thebump. https://www.thebump.com/a/how-did-baby-food-become-a-household-staple
15. Solid Starts. (2021, October 27). *The History of Baby Food - How Do We Feed Babies?* https://solidstarts.com/baby-led-weaning/history-of-baby-food/
16. D'Auria, E. (2018, May 3). *Baby-led weaning: what a systematic review of the literature adds on.* Italian Journal of Pediatrics. https://ijponline.biomedcentral.com/

articles/10.1186/s13052-018-0487-8

17. Sachs, M. (2011). *Baby-led weaning and current UK recommendations,are they compatible?* Blackwell Publishing Ltd Maternal and Child Nutrition. https://onlinelibrary. wiley.com/doi/epdf/10.1111/j.1740-8709.2010.00278.x

18. Townsend, E. (2012, February 6). *Baby knows best? The impact of weaning style on food preferences and body mass index in early childhood in a case-controlled sample.* PubMed. https://pubmed.ncbi.nlm.nih.gov/22315302/

19. Brown, A. (2015, February 1). *Early influences on child satietyâ□□responsiveness: the role of weaning style.* Wiley Online Library. https://onlinelibrary.wiley.com/doi/10. 1111/j.2047-6310.2013.00207.x

20. Morison, B. (2018, August 1). *Impact of a Modified Version of Baby-Led Weaning on Dietary Variety and Food Preferences in Infants.* PubMed Central (PMC). https://www. ncbi.nlm.nih.gov/pmc/articles/PMC6115843/

21. Lin, S. (2018, September 21). *The Complete Guide to Baby Led Weaning.* Dr Steven Lin. https://www.drstevenlin.com/baby-led-weaning-guide/

22. Patel, O. (2021, August 27). *Baby Led Weaning: All the Benefits, and How to Prepare.* The Everymom. https://theeverymom.com/baby-led-weaning/

23. WeaningWorld. (2021, April 20). *An introduction to Sensory Weaning.* Weaningworld.Com. https://weaningworld.com/an-introduction-to-sensory-weaning/

24. Morison, B. J. (2016, May 1). *How different are baby-led weaning and conventional complementary feeding? A cross-sectional study of infants aged 6–8 months.* BMJ Open. https://bmjopen.bmj.com/content/6/5/e010665

25. Hammons, A. J. (2011, June 1). *Is Frequency of Shared Family Meals Related to the Nutritional Health of Children and Adolescents?* American Academy of Pediatrics. https://pediatrics.aappublications.org/content/127/6/e1565

26. Fangupo, L. J. (2016, October 1). *A Baby-Led Approach to Eating Solids and Risk of Choking.* American Academy of Pediatrics. https://pediatrics.aappublications.org/ content/138/4/e20160772

27. Brown, A. (2018, August 1). *No difference in self-reported frequency of choking between infants introduced to solid foods using a baby-led weaning or traditional spoon-feeding approach.* Wiley Online Library. https://onlinelibrary.wiley.com/doi/full/10.1111/jhn. 12528

28. Morison, B. J. (2016, May 1). *How different are baby-led weaning and conventional complementary feeding? A cross-sectional study of infants aged 6–8 months.* BMJ Open. https://bmjopen.bmj.com/content/6/5/e010665

29. Dogan, E. (2018, December 1). *Baby led complementary feeding: Randomized controlled study.* Wiley Online Library. https://onlinelibrary.wiley.com/doi/abs/10.1111/ ped.13671

30. Bushell, S. (2021, April 29). *Weaning Premature Babies - discover the really important factors you need to know.* Weaning | Fussy Eating | The Children's Nutritionist. https://www.childrensnutrition.co.uk/full-blog/weaning-premature-babies

31. J. Coll (2019, October 25). *Why is Baby Led Weaning (BLW) not for all babies?* Jessica's Baby Led Weaning Blog. https://jessicacoll.com/blog/why-is-blw-not-for-all-babies/

32. Jill Rabin. (2018). *Transitioning Your Baby to Solids Using the Baby-Led Weaning Approach.* NADS Conference. https://www.nads.org/wp-content/uploads/2018/08/Rabin-NADS-ConferenceTransitioning-Your-Baby-to-Solids-Using-the-BLW-Approach.pdf

2. Eliminate the Rules!

1. D'Andrea, R. (2021, October 30). *Can You Combine Purees and Baby Led Weaning?* | *New Ways Nutrition.* New Ways Nutrition | Pediatric Dietitian Focusing on Infant and Toddler Nutrition with a Focus on Starting Solid Foods. https://newwaysnutrition.com/babies/combine-traditional-baby-led-weaning/
2. Stasenko, N. R. D. (2021, September 26). *Starting Solids: Can I combine BLW and spoon feeding?* Feeding Bytes. https://feedingbytes.com/2017/10/can-i-combine-blw-and-spoon-feeding-when-starting-solids/
3. Stasenko, N. R. D. (2021, September 26). *Starting Solids: Can I combine BLW and spoon feeding?* Feeding Bytes. https://feedingbytes.com/2017/10/can-i-combine-blw-and-spoon-feeding-when-starting-solids/
4. Abrams, E. M. (2015, November 17). *Food introduction and allergy prevention in infants.* PubMed Central (PMC). https://www.ncbi.nlm.nih.gov/pmc/articles/PMC4646750/
5. Morison, B. (2018, August 1). *Impact of a Modified Version of Baby-Led Weaning on Dietary Variety and Food Preferences in Infants.* PubMed Central (PMC). https://www.ncbi.nlm.nih.gov/pmc/articles/PMC6115843/
6. Poulton, T. (2020, November 15). *Can you combine spoon-feeding and baby-led weaning?* Baby Led Weaning Tribe. https://www.babyledweaningtribe.com/can-you-combine-spoon-feeding-and-baby-led-weaning/
7. Cameron, S. L. (2012, November 1). *How Feasible Is Baby-Led Weaning as an Approach to Infant Feeding? A Review of the Evidence.* PubMed Central (PMC). https://www.ncbi.nlm.nih.gov/pmc/articles/PMC3509508/
8. UNICEF. (2016, October). *RESPONSIVE FEEDING: SUPPORTING CLOSE AND LOVING RELATIONSHIPS.* The Baby Friendly Initiative. https://www.unicef.org.uk/babyfriendly/wp-content/uploads/sites/2/2017/12/Responsive-Feeding-Infosheet-Unicef-UK-Baby-Friendly-Initiative.pdf
9. *SPOON FEEDING BASICS* (Section 1.6). (2019). Holt International. https://www.holtinternational.org/about/child-nutrition/feeding-and-positioning-manual/pdfs/part-1/chapter-1-section-6-spoon-feeding-basics.pdf
10. Judy & Megan. (2017). *Smarter Spoon-Feeding.* Feeding Littles. https://www.feedinglittles.com/blog/five-spoon-feeding-mistakes-most-parents-make
11. *Sequence of Development and Feeding Skills in Healthy, Full-Term Infants.* (2017). Right Start Services. https://www.rightstartservices.com/wp-content/uploads/2017/04/Sequence-of-Development-and-Feeding-Skills.pdf

3. When and How to Get Ready

1. Ben-Joseph, E. (2018). *Breastfeeding FAQs: Solids and Supplementing (for Parents) - Nemours KidsHealth.* Kids Health. https://kidshealth.org/en/parents/breastfeed-solids.html
2. *Starting Solid Foods.* (2021). HealthyChildren.Org. https://www.healthychildren.org/English/ages-stages/baby/feeding-nutrition/Pages/Starting-Solid-Foods.aspx
3. Harris, G. (2017). *Are There Sensitive Periods for Food Acceptance in Infancy?* PubMed Central (PMC). https://www.ncbi.nlm.nih.gov/pmc/articles/PMC5438435/
4. Shaw, G. (2013, September 22). *Starting Solid Foods.* WebMD. https://www.webmd.com/parenting/baby/starting-solid-food
5. Shaw, G. (2013, September 22). *Starting Solid Foods.* WebMD. https://www.webmd.com/parenting/baby/starting-solid-food
6. Shaw, G. (2013, September 22). *Starting Solid Foods.* WebMD. https://www.webmd.

com/parenting/baby/starting-solid-food

7. *Corrected Age For Preemies.* (2018). HealthyChildren.Org. https://www.healthychildren.org/English/ages-stages/baby/preemie/Pages/Corrected-Age-For-Preemies.aspx

8. *Baby led weaning - Family Lives.* (2021). Family Lives. https://www.familylives.org.uk/advice/pregnancy-and-baby/feeding/weaning/

9. NHS website. (2021, May 26). *Your baby's first solid foods.* Nhs.Uk. https://www.nhs.uk/conditions/baby/weaning-and-feeding/babys-first-solid-foods/

10. NHS website. (2021, May 26). *Your baby's first solid foods.* Nhs.Uk. https://www.nhs.uk/conditions/baby/weaning-and-feeding/babys-first-solid-foods/

11. Olivier, M. (2019, April 4). *Transitioning from Purees to Solids.* Baby Foode. https://babyfoode.com/blog/transitioning-from-purees-to-solids/

12. Palanjian, A. (2021, June 7). *Ultimate Guide to Baby Led Weaning (and Best First Foods).* Yummy Toddler Food. https://www.yummytoddlerfood.com/first-foods-for-baby/

13. Huhn, J. (2020, August 28). *Guide to Gagging Vs. Choking During Baby Weaning |ReadySetFood – Ready, Set, Food!* Ready.Set.Food. https://readysetfood.com/blogs/community/gagging-vs-choking-during-baby-weaning-how-to-tell-the-difference

14. Solid Starts. (2021, September 23). *Babies Gagging When Starting Solids.* https://solidstarts.com/starting-solids/safety/gagging/

15. Huhn, J. (2020, August 28). *Guide to Gagging Vs. Choking During Baby Weaning |ReadySetFood – Ready, Set, Food!* Ready.Set.Food. https://readysetfood.com/blogs/community/gagging-vs-choking-during-baby-weaning-how-to-tell-the-difference

16. Huhn, J. (2020, August 28). *Guide to Gagging Vs. Choking During Baby Weaning |ReadySetFood – Ready, Set, Food!* Ready.Set.Food. https://readysetfood.com/blogs/community/gagging-vs-choking-during-baby-weaning-how-to-tell-the-difference

17. Solid Starts. (2021, September 23). *Babies Gagging When Starting Solids.* https://solidstarts.com/starting-solids/safety/gagging/

18. Huhn, J. (2020, August 28). *Guide to Gagging Vs. Choking During Baby Weaning |ReadySetFood – Ready, Set, Food!* Ready.Set.Food. https://readysetfood.com/blogs/community/gagging-vs-choking-during-baby-weaning-how-to-tell-the-difference

19. Huhn, J. (2020, August 28). *Guide to Gagging Vs. Choking During Baby Weaning |ReadySetFood – Ready, Set, Food!* Ready.Set.Food. https://readysetfood.com/blogs/community/gagging-vs-choking-during-baby-weaning-how-to-tell-the-difference

20. *Choking Rescue for Babies.* (2020). HealthLink BC. https://www.healthlinkbc.ca/health-topics/tf7236

21. Motroni, A. (2021, March 6). *10 Best High Chairs for Baby-Led Weaning (BLW).* The Postpartum Party. https://thepostpartumparty.com/best-high-chair-baby-led-weaning/

22. NHS Forth Valley. (2014). *A Guide to Weaning.* NHS. https://nhsforthvalley.com/wp-content/uploads/2014/03/A-guide-to-weaning-April2014.pdf

23. *SPOON FEEDING BASICS* (Section 1.6). (2019). Holt International. https://www.holtinternational.org/about/child-nutrition/feeding-and-positioning-manual/pdfs/part-1/chapter-1-section-6-spoon-feeding-basics.pdf

24. *SPOON FEEDING BASICS* (Section 1.6). (2019). Holt International. https://www.holtinternational.org/about/child-nutrition/feeding-and-positioning-manual/pdfs/part-1/chapter-1-section-6-spoon-feeding-basics.pdf

25. *How do we get started with solids?* (2018, January 2). KellyMom.Com. https://kellymom.com/nutrition/starting-solids/solids-how/

4. How to Prepare a Meal

1. Pas, M. (2020, November 28). *How to Cut Foods for Baby Led Weaning*. BLW Guides |. https://masandpas.com/baby-led-weaning/
2. Ferraro, K. (2021, May 6). *5 Day Baby Food Texture Challenge*. Fortified Family. https://www.fortifiedfam.com/home/2017/6/13/5-day-baby-food-texture-challenge
3. *Salt and Health*. (2003). The Stationery Office. https://assets.publishing.service.gov.uk/government/uploads/system/uploads/attachment_data/file/338782/SACN_Salt_and_Health_report.pdf
4. Forestell, C. A. (2017). *Flavor Perception and Preference Development in Human Infants*. PubMed. https://pubmed.ncbi.nlm.nih.gov/28903110/
5. A. (2020, June 19). *A guide to baby weaning with herbs and spices*. Seasoned Pioneers. https://www.seasonedpioneers.com/a-guide-to-baby-weaning-with-herbs-and-spices/
6. Health Canada. (2021). *Food safety information for children ages 5 and under - Canada.ca*. Canada. https://www.canada.ca/en/health-canada/services/food-safety-vulnerable-populations/food-safety-information-children-ages-5-under.html
7. Davis, C. M., MD. (1928, October 1). *SELF SELECTION OF DIET BY NEWLY WEANED INFANTS: AN EXPERIMENTAL STUDY*. JAMA Pediatrics | JAMA Network.https://jamanetwork.com/journals/jamapediatrics/article-abstract/1718986
8. *MyPlate | U.S. Department of Agriculture*. (2020). MyPlate. https://www.myplate.gov/
9. *Babies and Toddlers Need Iron to Thrive*. (n.d.). Stanford Children's Health. https://www.stanfordchildrens.org/en/topic/default?id=babies-and-toddlers-need-iron-to-thrive-1-4100
10. Brooks, R. (2021, April 18). *Your ultimate guide to iron intake and iron deficiency anemia*. Movement and Nutrition. https://www.movementandnutrition.co.uk/iron-intake-and-iron-deficiency-anemia/
11. *FoodData Central*. (2021). USDA. https://fdc.nal.usda.gov/
12. Lynch, S. R. (1980). *Interaction of vitamin C and iron*. PubMed. https://pubmed.ncbi.nlm.nih.gov/6940487/
13. Lönnerdal, B. (2010). *Calcium and iron absorption--mechanisms and public health relevance*. PubMed. https://pubmed.ncbi.nlm.nih.gov/21462112/#
14. Lönnerdal, B. (2010). *Calcium and iron absorption--mechanisms and public health relevance*. PubMed. https://pubmed.ncbi.nlm.nih.gov/21462112/#
15. *Iron-Deficiency Anemia in Children*. (n.d.). Cedars Sinai. https://www.cedars-sinai.org/health-library/diseases-and-conditions---pediatrics/i/iron-deficiency-anemia-in-children.html
16. *Food Allergies | Healthy Schools | CDC*. (n.d.). CDC. https://www.cdc.gov/healthyschools/foodallergies/index.htm
17. *What Is a Food Allergy?* (n.d.). Food Allergy Research & Education. https://www.foodallergy.org/resources/what-food-allergy
18. Center for Food Safety and Applied Nutrition. (2018, July 16). *Food Allergen Labeling And Consumer Protection Act of 2004 Questions and Answers*. U.S. Food and Drug Administration. https://www.fda.gov/food/food-allergensgluten-free-guidance-documents-regulatory-information/food-allergen-labeling-and-consumer-protection-act-2004-questions-and-answers
19. Koplin, J. J. (2010). *Can early introduction of egg prevent egg allergy in infants? A population-based study*. PubMed. https://pubmed.ncbi.nlm.nih.gov/20920771/
20. Ierodiakonou, D., MD PhD. (2016, September 20). *Timing of Allergenic Food Introduction to the Infant Diet and Risk of Allergic or Autoimmune Disease: A*. Jama Network. https://jamanetwork.com/journals/jama/fullarticle/2553447

21. DGA. (2020). *Dietary Guidelines for Americans*. https://www.dietaryguidelines.gov/sites/default/files/2020-12/Dietary_Guidelines_for_Americans_2020-2025.pdf
22. Conway, M., MD. (2021, July 21). *This is the best way to introduce allergens to babies.* Today's Parent. https://www.todaysparent.com/baby/baby-health/introducing-allergens-to-babies-how-to/
23. Marcin, A. (2021, March 25). *What to Do If Your Baby Has an Allergic Reaction to Food.* Healthline. https://www.healthline.com/health/baby/baby-allergic-reaction-to-food#seek-emergency-help
24. Conway, M., MD. (2021, July 21). *This is the best way to introduce allergens to babies.* Today's Parent. https://www.todaysparent.com/baby/baby-health/introducing-allergens-to-babies-how-to/
25. Thompson, A. (2019, May 27). *Three Puree Textures to Try.* Ezpz. https://ezpzfun.com/blogs/feeding-tips/three-puree-textures-to-try
26. Kuzemchak, M. S. S. (2020, March 30). *Understanding Baby Food Stages: A Cheat Sheet for.* Parents. https://www.parents.com/baby/feeding/nutrition/baby-food-stages-and-steps-by-age/
27. Pediatric Partners. (2021). *FEEDING YOUR 4 MONTH OLD.* https://pediatricpartnerskc.com/Education/Feeding/FEEDING-YOUR-4-MONTH-OL

5. Game Time!

1. Rapley, Gill; Murkett, Tracey. Baby-Led Weaning, Completely Updated and Expanded Tenth Anniversary Edition: The Essential Guide—How to Introduce Solid Foods and Help Your Baby to Grow Up a Happy and Confident Eater (p. 84). The Experiment. Kindle Edition.
2. Rapley, Gill; Murkett, Tracey. Baby-Led Weaning, Completely Updated and Expanded Tenth Anniversary Edition: The Essential Guide—How to Introduce Solid Foods and Help Your Baby to Grow Up a Happy and Confident Eater (p. 84). The Experiment. Kindle Edition.
3. Rapley, Gill; Murkett, Tracey. Baby-Led Weaning, Completely Updated and Expanded Tenth Anniversary Edition: The Essential Guide—How to Introduce Solid Foods and Help Your Baby to Grow Up a Happy and Confident Eater (p. 84). The Experiment. Kindle Edition.
4. A. (2021, August 9). *Responsive feeding: recognizing hunger and fullness cues.* My Little Eater. https://mylittleeater.com/responsive-feeding/
5. *Signs Your Child is Hungry or Full.* (2021, July 22). Centers for Disease Control and Prevention. https://www.cdc.gov/nutrition/infantandtoddlernutrition/mealtime/signs-your-child-is-hungry-or-full.html
6. Solid Starts. (2021, July 21). *Food Sizes & Shapes to Serve Baby at Each Age.* https://solidstarts.com/starting-solids/safety/safe-food-sizes-shapes-for-babies/
7. Sharda, J. R. P. N. D. (2020, July 15). *How to Encourage the Pincer Grasp.* Happy Healthy Eaters. https://happyhealthyeaters.com/how-to-encourage-the-pincer-grasp/
8. Solid Starts. (2021, July 21). *Food Sizes & Shapes to Serve Baby at Each Age.* https://solidstarts.com/starting-solids/safety/safe-food-sizes-shapes-for-babies/
9. Clark, J. (n.d.). *Will my baby's poo be different with baby-led weaning?* Baby Centre. https://www.babycentre.co.uk/x25022998/will-my-babys-poo-be-different-with-baby-led-weaning
10. Muth, N. D. (2019). *Recommended Drinks for Young Children Ages 0–5.* HealthyChildren.Org. https://www.healthychildren.org/English/healthy-living/nutrition/Pages/Recommended-Drinks-for-Young-Children-Ages-0-5.aspx

11. Graybill, R. (2018, October 8). *What About Sippy Cups?* TEIS, Inc. https://teisinc.com/blog/what-about-sippy-cups/
12. Edwena (2021, October 22). *Open Cup Drinking 101: How to teach open cup drinking to your baby.* My Little Eater. https://mylittleeater.com/opencupdrinking/
13. Mot, A. O. G. (2021, May 24). *How to Teach Your Baby to Drink from a Straw - Your Kid's Table.* Your Kid's Table. https://yourkidstable.com/how-to-teach-your-baby-or-toddler-to/

6. What to Offer Based on Age and Skill Level

1. Solid Starts. (2021, November 3). *Babies Gagging When Starting Solids.* https://solidstarts.com/starting-solids/safety/gagging/
2. Sharda, J. R. P. N. D. (2021, October 1). *Help! My Baby is Stuffing Food!* Happy Healthy Eaters. https://happyhealthyeaters.com/baby-stuffing-food/
3. Solid Starts. (2021, August 24). *Chicken Liver for Babies - First Foods for Baby.* https://solidstarts.com/foods/chicken-liver/
4. *Baby-Led Weaning: What You Need to Know.* (2021, October 27). Cleveland Clinic. https://health.clevelandclinic.org/baby-led-weaning/

7. Baby-Led Weaning for the Busy Parent

1. Cohen, J. (2017, July 19). *Kids & Treats: How Much is Too Much?* Dr Jennifer Cohen. https://www.drjennifercohen.com/kids-treats/
2. Edwena, A. (2021, August 3). *Top 3 Strategies for Serving Dessert to Kids.* My Little Eater. https://mylittleeater.com/top-3-strategies-for-serving-dessert-to-kids/

8. Easy Three-Ingredient Recipes

1. Olivier, M. (2021, October 21). *3-Ingredient Banana Pancakes for Baby.* Baby Foode. https://babyfoode.com/blog/banana-pancakes-for-baby/
2. H. (2021, August 12). *3 Ingredient Cheddar Broccoli Egg Muffins.* Fit Mama Real Food. https://www.fitmamarealfood.com/cheddar-broccoli-egg-muffin/
3. Olivier, M. (2021b, July 16). *Healthy Yogurt Fruit Popsicles (8 Fun Flavors!).* Baby Foode. https://babyfoode.com/blog/yogurt-popsicles-for-toddlers-kids/
4. Baby Led Feeding. (2021, January 25). *Salmon Fish Cakes with Avocado and Yogurt & Lime Dressing.* https://www.babyledfeeding.com/recipe/salmon-fish-cakes-avocado-yogurt-lime-dressing/
5. Olivier, M. (2021a, February 23). *Baked Seasoned Tofu Nuggets.* Baby Foode. https://babyfoode.com/blog/baked-seasoned-tofu-nuggets/
6. Martin, S. (2020, December 10). *Authentic Hummus (3 Ingredients).* Shane & Simple. https://shaneandsimple.com/classic-hummus/
7. Mph Rd, K. S. (2020, December 7). *3-Ingredient Pulled Pork Instant Pot.* Hungry Hobby. https://hungryhobby.net/3-ingredient-pulled-pork-instant-pot/
8. M. (2021b, August 7). *3 Ingredient Banana Cookies for Babies.* MJ and Hungryman. https://www.mjandhungryman.com/banana-oatmeal-cookies/
9. J. (2020, July 7). *3 ingredient yogurt cake (suitable from 6 months+).* WEANINGFUL. https://weaningful.com/3-ingredient-yogurt-cake-suitable-from-6-months/
10. A. (2021, January 14). *Porridge Fingers.* Healthy Little Foodies. https://www.healthylittlefoodies.com/porridge-fingers/

9. Healthy Meal Plans & Schedules

1. Marygrace, T. (2021, January 25). *Baby-Led Weaning*. What to Expect. https://www.whattoexpect.com/first-year/feeding-baby/baby-led-weaning/
2. Marygrace, T. (2021, June 11). *Baby Feeding Schedule and Food Chart for the First Year*. What to Expect. https://www.whattoexpect.com/first-year/feeding-baby/how-to-get-baby-on-feeding-schedule/
3. Simkins, D. (2021, January 15). *Baby Led Weaning Sample Feeding Schedules*. Family Style Nutrition. http://www.familystylenutrition.com/baby-led-weaning-sample-feeding-schedules/

10. Common Mistakes and Questions

1. Judy & Megan. (2017). *Smarter Spoon-Feeding*. Feeding Littles. https://www.feedinglittles.com/blog/five-spoon-feeding-mistakes-most-parents-make
2. J. (2019, December 11). *Can you switch to BLW? Can you do a bit of both?* Jessica's Baby Led Weaning Blog. https://jessicacoll.com/blog/can-switch-blw-can-do-bit-both/
3. Dubinsky, D. D. (2021). *Age-by-age guide to feeding your baby*. Babycenter. https://www.babycenter.com/baby/solids-finger-foods/age-by-age-guide-to-feeding-your-baby_1400680
4. Fangupo, L. J. (2016). *A Baby-Led Approach to Eating Solids and Risk of Choking*. Pubmed. https://pubmed.ncbi.nlm.nih.gov/27647715/
5. Marcin, A. (2018, June 28). *What Is Extrusion Reflex?* Healthline. https://www.healthline.com/health/parenting/extrusion-reflex
6. Coulthard, H. (2009). *Delayed introduction of lumpy foods to children during the complementary feeding period affects child's food acceptance and feeding at 7 years of age*. Pubmed. https://pubmed.ncbi.nlm.nih.gov/19161546/
7. Forestel, C. A. (2007). *Early Determinants of Fruit and Vegetable Acceptance*. NCBI. https://www.ncbi.nlm.nih.gov/pmc/articles/PMC2268898/
8. https://www.familyeducation.com/life/starting-solids/how-tell-if-your-baby-likes-new-food
9. Khan, A. (2021, October 30). *Gagging in Babies - Is it Normal?* FirstCry Parenting. https://parenting.firstcry.com/articles/baby-gagging-things-you-need-to-know/
10. *Salt Intake Guidelines for Babies — Little Gourmet - Baby Led Weaning Guide*. (n.d.). Little Gourmet. https://littlegourmetbaby.com/salt-intake-guidelines-for-babies
11. Desiraju, M. (2018). *When Can My Baby Start Drinking Juice? (for Parents) - Nemours KidsHealth*. Kids Health. https://kidshealth.org/en/parents/babies-juice.html
12. Health Jade Team. (2019, December 2). *Neophobia*. Health Jade. https://healthjade.net/neophobia/
13. *Arsenic in Infant Rice Cereal*. (n.d.). Healthy Babies Bright Futures. https://www.hbbf.org/arsenic-infant-rice-cereal
14. Greene, A., MD. (2010). *Aversion to Solids*. DrGreene.Com. https://www.drgreene.com/qa-articles/aversion-solids
15. Stasenko Ms, R. N. D. (2020, March 17). *How One Mom Embraced Both Baby-Led Weaning and Purees*. Parents. https://www.parents.com/recipes/scoop-on-food/should-babies-skip-purees-5-things-i-learned-about-baby-led-weaning/